Praise for

PARENT THE CHILD YOU *Have,*
NOT THE CHILD YOU *Were*

"This rare book is a godsend for every parent. Finally, there is a book that deals straightforwardly with a rampant family issue: the unwitting influence of the parent's childhood on how they raise their own children. In an age of overemphasis on tools and techniques, Dr. Turns-Coe turns her attention to where it can do the most good: helping the parent to understand their own motives and to single out their children's real needs from the noise of family life. No parent wants to cause problems for their children, and this practical, wise book will show you easy ways of ensuring that your child feels loved, understood, and safely guided. A fantastic contribution to parents everywhere—I heartily recommend this book."

—**Lindsay C. Gibson, PsyD,** licensed clinical psychologist and best-selling author of *Adult Children of Emotionally Immature Parents* and *Recovering from Emotionally Immature Parents*

"Every parent should read this book! Dr. Turns-Coe reveals a proven path to healthy parenting, and her writing is chock-full of practical strategies and profound wisdom. Don't miss out on this invaluable message."

—**Drs. Les & Leslie Parrott,** #1 *New York Times* best-selling authors of *Saving Your Marriage Before It Starts*

"Parent the Child You Have, Not the Child You Were is a book that is long overdue. As a pediatrician, I have personally witnessed thousands of kids raised by parents who were profoundly, but subconsciously, influenced by their childhoods. Every parent does this—no matter how well-intentioned they are. I did it, and I would have loved to have had this book when my kids were young. I also would have given it to every one of the parents in my practice. It is that important."

—**Meg Meeker, MD,** best-selling author of *Strong Fathers, Strong Daughters*

"There's never been a better time to invest in loving and skillful parenting, as young people experience an alarming mental health crisis. In this wise and timely book, Dr. Brie Turns-Coe shares evidence-based practices that will help you to heal from your past so you can parent in the present."

—**Seth Gillihan, PhD,** licensed psychologist and author of *Mindful Cognitive Behavioral Therapy* and *The CBT Deck*

"*Parent the Child You Have, Not the Child You Were* is a great tool for parents to build healthy, attachment-based relationships with their kids! Focusing on attuning to your child by recognizing and meeting their needs builds trust. Our children then feel safe to come to us, as parents, because they feel seen, heard, and understood. By walking a healing path for ourselves, we become the parents that our children most need. This book is a great guide for that journey!"

—**Christina Reese, PhD,** author of *Attachment: 60 Trauma-Informed Assessment and Treatment Interventions Across the Lifespan*

"Dr. Brie Turns-Coe takes an honest perspective to parenting, focusing on what matters most: forming a healthy connection with your child. Her book offers tools to help you pause and reflect on your needs in order to build a stronger, meaningful relationship with your child. You will learn to be patient, present, and connected. This is a must-read!"

—**Lisa Weed Phifer, D.Ed., NCSP,** author of *The CBT Toolbox for Young Adults* and *Trauma-Informed Social-Emotional Toolbox for Children & Adolescents*

"What if the way to become the parent you need to be today starts with a deep dive into where you started—with how *you* were parented? Dr. Brie wisely illustrates an upside-down way of getting things right side up in your home. *Parent the Child You Have, Not the Child You Were* is a book you'll find yourself reading from cover to cover. I highly recommend this book to strengthen your own heart and mind, and as a powerful way to bless your children."

—**John Trent, PhD,** president of StrongFamilies and The Center for Strong Families and author of *The Blessing* and *Where Do I Go from Here?*

"*Parent the Child You Have, Not the Child You Were* is an excellent introduction to how our past can impact our present self, and the implications of that for parenting. Dr. Turns-Coe does a masterful job of explaining how negative core beliefs, past trauma, and even aspirational goals can pull a parent's focus away from the child in front of them. The true-to-life case examples and reflection prompts throughout this book will help parents open their eyes to how their past is influencing their parenting—and what they can do about it."

—**Robyn Koslowitz, PhD,** host of the *Post-Traumatic Parenting* podcast

PARENT
THE CHILD YOU
Have, NOT THE
CHILD YOU *Were*

Break Generational Patterns.
Raise Thriving Kids.

Brie Turns-Coe, PhD, LMFT, ASDCS

Published by
PESI Publishing, Inc.
3839 White Ave
Eau Claire, WI 54703

Cover and Interior Design: Emily Dyer
Editing: Chelsea Thompson and Jenessa Jackson, PhD

ISBN: 9781683736417 (print)
ISBN: 9781683736424 (ePUB)
ISBN: 9781683736431 (ePDF)

Printed in the United States of America.

PESI Publishing
pesipublishing.com

Dedication

I'd like to first dedicate this book to my parents. Although they parented me from their past, they supported, encouraged, and strengthened me to become the person I am today. Without them, none of this would be possible.

I'd also like to dedicate this book to each of you. Thank you all!

About the Author

Brie Turns-Coe, PHD, LMFT, ASDCS, is an associate professor of marriage and family therapy at Arizona Christian University and the director of the Master of Marriage and Family Therapy program. Dr. Turns-Coe has presented at local, state, national, and international conferences on parenting and published extensively on the topic of family therapy. She also coedited the text *Systemically Treating Autism* (Routledge, 2019) and wrote the children's book *I Will Always Love You.*

While treating families struggling to manage children's undesirable behaviors, Dr. Turns-Coe began asking the parents about their reflections on their children's behaviors and focusing on the parents' needs. Most parents had fears that were being triggered when interacting with their children—fear that they weren't "good enough" parents, fear that they were just like their own parents, and fear that they would be hated by their children. When the parents' primary fears and traumas were treated, their parenting drastically improved, and so did their children's behaviors.

Dr. Turns-Coe has treated hundreds of parents who were parenting through their past traumas and helped them achieve healing and strengthen their relationships. To learn more about her work and read success stories from other parents, visit her at www.drbrieturns.com or follow her on social media (@thefamilytherapist).

Contents

Activities

Acknowledgments

I would like to start by thanking my Lord and Savior, who taught me the true meaning of grace and what it means to heal from trauma for the next generation.

Additionally, I would like to thank each client who learned how to parent the child they have and healed from years of pain. Every family, parent, and child I have seen since 2012 has contributed in some way to the creation of this book.

I'd also like to thank several colleagues, friends, and mentors who encouraged me while writing this book or provided support during my career—specifically Scott Sibley, Carolyn Pela, Brandon Eddy, Deborah Pettitt and the team at Family Christian Counseling Center, Sara Jordan, Joe Wetchler, Lorna Hecker, and Rachael Olufowote. Thank you, Paul Springer, for challenging me to be a better therapist, writer, academic, and person. I will never forget the hours you have spent guiding and inspiring me.

Finally, I'd like to thank my husband, who has been my rock during this writing and publication process: Zachary Coe. You're my best friend, and I cannot wait to embark on our next journey together.

Introduction

Raising a child is one of the most challenging and exhausting jobs in the world. You often find yourself wondering if you are a good enough parent, if you are doing the right thing for your child, if your child is intentionally driving you to distraction. There are thousands of parenting books that teach you how to raise an amazing child, become a calmer parent, and avoid becoming the parent who raised you. However, these books don't address a widespread phenomenon I've observed while providing family therapy to hundreds of struggling parents across America over the past decade. I've come to recognize one of the most common mistakes parents make: unintentionally parenting the child they *were*, not the child they *have*.

Most of these parents tell me, "I won't raise my children the way I was raised." At face value, it's hard to find anything wrong with this perspective. But I've seen how this mindset can seriously damage the relationship these parents have with their children. Why? Because it encourages the parent to focus on themselves instead of their child.

Regardless of how fondly (or not) you remember your childhood, your past experiences may be dictating how you raise your child. *Parenting through your past*, as I call it, happens when a parent subconsciously makes decisions or engages in certain behaviors based on the child they used to be, not the child they have in front of them. Consider statements like the following:

"I refuse to tell my child 'Because I said so.' My parents never explained anything to me, so I attempt to give my child a logical explanation for the decisions I make."

1

"I'm teaching my child the value of hard work because my parents gave me everything I wanted. As an adult, I'm figuring out that's not how the world works. I don't buy my kids a ton of clothes and toys; they have to earn it."

"I'm going to do the opposite of everything my parents did."

These declarations reflect the reality that many parents raise their children in response to or in reaction against the mentality their own parents had when they were growing up. Childhood memories, both good and bad, frequently impact how a parent instructs, interacts with, and bonds with their child. Although the quotes above do not come from an uncaring or unloving place, they are signs that someone is parenting based on experiences in their own past, rather than tuning into what their child needs here and now.

A caregiver who is parenting through their past does this for one of two reasons. First, some parents make decisions in an effort to satisfy their own unmet core needs from childhood. Lincoln, the father of a twelve-year-old son, frequently bought his child the newest video games even though his wife strongly disapproved. His rationale: "My parents never understood how hard it was for me when I didn't fit in at school. I won't let my son feel excluded by his peers."

Second, parents often fear that their child will experience uncomfortable or difficult challenges, thoughts, or feelings similar to what the parent experienced as a child. Kelly, the mother of a sixteen-year-old daughter, refused to let her daughter attend sleepovers and birthday parties. When asked about her thoughts in session, Kelly responded, "Kids can get into so much trouble when left alone. I don't want her in a situation in which she could be tempted to use drugs or drink, like I did."

At first glance, these may seem like protective or even loving responses. However, in both cases the parent was not tuning into their child's need for essential experiences that help them learn, grow, and develop their identity. Instead, they were trying to fulfill their own unmet needs or avoid the danger of their child making a harmful decision. If you attempt to prevent or guard your child against uncomfortable emotions, you're not allowing them to build resilience and character. As a result, your child will struggle not only with making decisions, but also with finding their own values and morals.

Everyone has different core needs; if you unknowingly make parenting decisions to satisfy *your* unmet needs, your child's needs are not being met. This often leads to a child lashing out in an attempt to get their needs met, whether it be through tantrums (toddlers), substance use (adolescents), or risky sexual activity (teens). These negative behaviors eventually drive the parent to seek therapy for their child, which in turn led me, after 10 years as a marriage and family therapist, to identify this negative parenting style.

Who I Am

Since 2011, I have treated individuals, couples, and families struggling with children who are lashing out, withdrawing, or making harmful choices. Despite the variety of individual factors in each parent-child relationship, I eventually noticed that every parent reflected a similar reason for raising their child a certain way: It was because of the parent's own childhood experiences.

Following this revelation, I set out to treat families by specifically focusing on parents, an approach that is highly debated in fields where the identified patient is the child. After learning about a parent's most noteworthy childhood memory and how they felt when it happened,

I would help them identify the core need within the memory that was not met. Every parent then responded, "This is exactly why I'm making the decisions I'm making. I'm protecting my child."

My question was always the same: "Protecting your child . . . or protecting *you* as a child?"

After wiping the tears away, the parents were ready to dive deep into their past and learn how their memories, core beliefs, and unmet needs were impacting their parenting. After many hours of therapy and hard work at home, these parents began drastically altering how they connected with their children. Years of pain, heartache, and unfulfilled needs were finally alleviated, which freed the parent to consciously see the child in front of them instead of their own reflection.

Knowing how common this parenting pattern is, I've written this book as a way to offer my knowledge for all parents to use at their own pace. As you begin, I have a few gentle reminders to help you get the most out of this book:

1. Engaging in self-reflection and learning about your past pain is hard. Sometimes it can be too hard. It's okay to take a break or seek professional help if needed.

2. You are *not* a bad parent. I am continuously asked this question by parents I'm in session with, and I always have the same answer: If you are seeking help, you're a good parent. In fact, seeking guidance so you can strengthen the relationship you have with your child makes you an incredibly caring parent.

3. There is no such thing as a perfect parent, so let it go. You will make mistakes in this process and often backslide, but don't worry—along with helping you change your negative parenting patterns, this book will teach you how to apologize

to your loved ones so you can transform mistakes into an even stronger connection.

Parenting the Child You Have

Parenting the child you have, also called parenting in the present, may seem like a basic and obvious parenting skill. However, it's very difficult to implement—hence, the many books that discuss how parents' past experiences influence how they raise their children and react to their behaviors. One of my favorites, *Parenting from the Inside Out* (Siegel & Hartzell, 2003), discusses how past traumas can alter the human brain and frame how we perceive and interact with our children. However, it's not only past traumas, but also the small disappointments and even the happy childhood events, that cause a person to parent from their past.

This book will teach you several novel concepts that can take the overwhelm out of parenting. First, you will learn to recognize how past events, both positive and negative, impact the way you parent. Second, you will learn how to heal from the negative experiences by identifying and fulfilling your unmet needs, and how you can hold on to the positive experiences of your childhood while allowing room to acknowledge that your child has their own unique needs. Third, you will learn to monitor the thoughts, responses, and shaming behaviors that contribute to parenting from your past. Finally, you will learn how to reconnect with your child by meeting their authentic needs, creating the relationship you have always longed for.

Whom This Book Is For

This book is primarily intended for parents who are struggling to address their child's problematic behaviors and nourish their relationship. My aim is to help these parents tune into their child's needs by acknowledging and healing their own unmet needs from the past.

In addition, this book is geared toward clinicians who are working with families in any capacity to change complicated parent-child relationship dynamics. When discussing the concept of parenting through your past with other clinicians, I was amazed at the responses I received. Many mental health clinicians disclosed seeing the same patterns in their therapy rooms but were unaware of how to help. For that reason, this book also includes information from the fields of cognitive neuroscience, marriage and family therapy, and trauma-informed care to provide therapists with the tools they need to help parents change ingrained patterns of behavior.

Finally, while writing this book, I discovered an additional audience I would like to reach: those healing from childhood trauma. One of my therapy specializations is trauma, which includes physical, emotional, psychological, and spiritual abuse. However, trauma isn't limited to "big" instances of abuse; it can include any experiences in which your core basic needs were not met. For example, when you were a child, your parent may have routinely missed your soccer games, told you they were busy when you asked for attention, insisted there was nothing to be upset about when you were crying, or placed you in time-out. Any of these experiences may have caused you trauma and pain because they left your core needs unmet. Whether you're already a parent or planning to become one, the concepts and tools in this book can help you heal long-standing childhood wounds and guide you toward happier, healthier relationships in the future.

How This Book Is Organized

As we begin this journey together, it's important to know what information we'll review.

Part 1 covers the concept of parenting through your past and outlines how you can identify when you are engaging in this parenting style. By highlighting education on brain development and how events during childhood impact a person's decision-making, chapter 1 introduces the notion of core beliefs and reveals how your past can impact your present via the brain's mechanisms for retaining memories and influencing future decisions. Chapter 2 provides various case scenarios that demonstrate the five common parenting styles people use when parenting through their past.

Part 2 reviews how parenting through your past can negatively impact your life in the present. Chapter 3 discusses how children can be negatively impacted by this parenting style, including key behaviors and phrases to look out for. It also examines how parenting through your past can damage relationships between siblings, with your spouse or partner, and even with yourself.

Part 3 provides education on how you can heal from your past pain. Chapter 4 will teach you how to self-soothe in times of stress, a vital tool for parenting. Chapter 5 then shows how you can sit with your past to identify what you currently need. Chapter 6 explains how to identify outward-facing core beliefs that may be impacting your self-esteem and, in turn, your parenting. Chapter 7 provides techniques to increase your self-confidence and replace your negative core beliefs with more positive and helpful beliefs.

Part 4 dives into a new parenting style: parenting the child you have. Chapter 8 explains how to replace parenting goals with parenting intentions that allow you to show up for your child in more effective ways. Chapter 9 discusses the impact of assumptions, comparisons, and labels on the parent-child relationship, while chapter 10 guides you in identifying your expectations for your child and adjusting them in a way that encourages your child's healthy autonomy and good decision-making. Chapter 11 focuses on how to make decisions, respond to challenging situations, and apologize to your child when you make mistakes. Chapter 12 deals with the important (but often overlooked) process of grieving the loss of the child (or childhood) you wish you had. Finally, chapter 13 teaches you how to meet your child's core psychological, emotional, and physical needs.

Final Note

An important note before you dive in: I'm not here to shame you. I truly believe that you are trying your best to develop the relationship you have always wanted with your child. This book isn't meant to critique your confusion or judge your past decisions. It's intended to help you discover a new, effective way to parent and, along the way, set you free from your past.

As you work to develop a deeper connection with your child, do not aim for perfection in your parenting—that simply doesn't exist. Instead, my hope is that this book adds to your toolbox and provides you with the encouragement and information you need to raise the next generation. Know also that this text isn't meant to be a one-and-done read. Healing and growing is a lifelong journey and will require reflection, adjustment, and apologies every step of the way. But you've got this. I'm right here with you.

—Dr. Brie

Part 1
—

Parenting Through Your Past

Chapter 1

—

Your Past Impacts
Your Present

Emily and Steve called me in a state of near desperation about their daughter Hailey. Despite their best efforts to raise her well, Hailey was becoming a textbook problem teen: rude, disrespectful, and condescending. Nothing they did—talking with her, grounding her, taking her phone and car keys—seemed to get through to her. "We are really struggling right now," Emily admitted on the phone. "My parents never would have let me behave this way, but I refuse to raise her the way my parents raised me. We just want a daughter who is kind and helpful. How do we fix this?"

After over a decade as a family therapist, I have heard thousands of parents ask the same question. Whether they're raising defiant teenagers, moody adolescents, or tantrum-prone toddlers, these exhausted parents have reached their limits trying to help their children but are still not sure what to do.

Regardless of the child or the undesirable behaviors they are showing, I always start family therapy by working with the parents. After all, the parents have more power to change the situation than the child does. Moreover, I've learned that very few parents are aware of what's happening below the surface of their parenting choices—specifically, the way that their own childhood is likely dictating how they interact with their child. Without realizing it, many parents are actually parenting the child they *were*, not the child they *have*.

No matter what your goal might be—to decrease your child's defiant behaviors, to increase the love and communication between you and your child, or simply to feel more confident in your parenting skills—learning how your past impacts your present is the first step toward changing the relationship you have with your child.

Parenting Through Your Past versus Parenting in the Present

It's not surprising that many of the parenting choices, responses, and decisions you make are based on your past experiences. Human beings learn by considering previously acquired knowledge and applying it to the current situation. For example, touching a hot stove when I was three years old helped me learn not to do that again! When it comes to parenting decisions, the previously gained information doesn't come from the latest research articles or the newest parenting books. It comes from how *you* were raised. These experiences dictate your current parenting decisions, causing you to parent through your past.

I intentionally use the word *dictate* here because there's a big difference between letting the past influence your parenting and letting it determine your entire approach. When you are influenced by your past, you can draw lessons from previous events and their outcomes while still being open to new ideas and information. But when you let the past dictate your parenting decisions, it prevents you from accepting and using new information, such as your child's unique needs, personality, and relationship with you. Recognizing this difference is crucial to understanding this book and positively altering your parenting.

So how do you know if your past experiences are dictating the way you parent? Here are a few indicators:

- When making a decision or responding to your child, you attempt to contradict negative core beliefs that were created during your childhood. For example, if you grew up feeling not good enough, your responses and choices will be fueled by an attempt to feel like a good enough parent.

- You struggle to stay emotionally regulated. If you frequently find yourself yelling, crying, having racing thoughts, or unable to think at all, your past is likely controlling how you're interpreting and analyzing current situations.

- You create goals and expectations for your child that are aimed at meeting your unmet needs or wounds. For example, perhaps you have a goal to raise happy, successful children in order to fulfill your unmet needs for family happiness and security.

- Your thoughts about your child—including any comparisons, labels, and assumptions you use to understand them—are rooted in what you experienced and how you behaved growing up. You might believe your child should achieve good grades in school because that's what your parents expected of you, or you might refuse to let your child start dating before a certain age because you believe your parents let you start dating too young.

As you learned in the introduction, parenting through your past occurs for two main reasons. First, it's an attempt to satisfy your unmet needs from childhood, and second, it's an effort to help your child avoid the uncomfortable challenges, thoughts, or feelings you experienced as a child. However, when you make a parenting decision that is skewed by your childhood experiences, the intention behind your response is in the wrong place. You're focused on what is best for you instead of what is best for your child.

In order to stop parenting from your past and begin parenting in the present, you must heal your own childhood wounds so you can identify, acknowledge, and fulfill your child's unique needs. When your intention is focused on what is best for your child, you can consider the information from your past experiences alongside current information you've gained about yourself and your child, empowering you to make better, more logical decisions that nourish the parent-child relationship you truly want.

Parenting in the present is one of the most challenging concepts I teach clients, due to how deeply ingrained your unmet needs are and how eager your brain is to have them met. In order to accurately identify what your child needs to grow and develop successfully, you must "rewire" your brain by acknowledging your past unmet needs and learning how to meet those needs yourself. While it will take a lot of practice and self-monitoring, you can heal from your past wounds and watch yourself turn into the parent your child needs, rather than the parent you wished had raised you. A key piece is acknowledging your past hurts and challenges and understanding how your memories of these experiences have shaped you into the person you are today.

Memories Make You Who You Are

Clare, a 52-year-old mother I worked with, described how she would sit on her grandmother's front porch, waiting for her mother to pick her up. "I would see her driving down the street as she visited people in our neighborhood, but she would never stop and see me," Clare remembered. "There were dozens of times she could have stopped, but she never did. I grew up thinking I wasn't wanted or loved by her . . . but Dr. Brie, it was 45 years ago. I forgive my mother for leaving me. I've healed from it, and it doesn't impact my life right now."

Like Clare, many of us can recall specific traumatic moments from our childhood but are quick to add, "It doesn't bother me anymore" or "My past has nothing to do with how I'm parenting my child." Actually, your past has everything to do with it! Your past informs how you view yourself, how you interpret your child's actions, and why you get upset by certain behaviors and emotions that your child displays. Regardless of whether you define your childhood as excellent, horrible, or somewhere in between, it's going to impact how you parent. After all, you learned how to parent—or how not to parent—from experiencing how your parents raised you.

Therefore, it's impossible to improve your parenting skills without first acknowledging how your childhood experiences have shaped who you are today. These experiences, and the feelings that arose from them, are embedded in your memories, which are among the most important aspects of your life and your sense of self. Both fond memories that bring joy, thankfulness, and a sense of fulfillment (last year's family vacation, your wedding day, the birth of your child) and memories full of pain, sadness, and disappointment (being bullied on the school playground, losing a loved one, being embarrassed in front of others) play a crucial part in how you think and behave today, as well as how you view yourself, other people, and your future.

Like a mirror, memories reflect your personal identity and sense of self-worth back to you. If many of your memories include feelings of fear, shame, guilt, or embarrassment, you'll typically view yourself in a negative light. Thoughts like *I'm not good enough*, *I'm a mistake*, *I'm not smart*, or *I'm not safe* may repeat themselves in your day-to-day life. Conversely, if most of your memories bring feelings of comfort, safety, and love, you probably view yourself positively, with thoughts like *I'm a good person, I'm loved, I'm valued,* or *I'm safe* replaying in your mind. These messages from your childhood memories are integrated into your current life story. For instance, Clare's early childhood memory helps explain why she currently fears not being loved or wanted by her children. Even though the event occurred more than 45 years ago, this vivid memory is incorporated into how she views herself today.

Experiences Create Your Core Beliefs

If I asked you to tell me about only one memory from your early childhood, what would you say? Waiting for a parent to pick you up from school and they never came? Asking for attention or comfort, only to have your parent start yelling at you? If you recalled a highly charged negative memory, you're not alone. Emotions are among the biggest factors that influence human memory storage and recall. Memories of highly negative emotional events are more vivid and are stored in the brain longer than memories of neutral events (Bowen et al., 2017). They even overpower memories involving positive emotions; the brain can recall negative events more accurately and quickly than positive ones (Canli et al., 2000). For example, someone may remember the car accident they were involved in as a four-year-old in much greater detail than the birthday party they had one month later. This is why most people—even those who perceive their childhood as great or their parents as loving—will mainly recall negative memories about their parents.

Although your childhood likely included many wonderful experiences as well, the negative experiences tend to be the ones that form your core beliefs. A core belief is a deeply held assumption, thought, or idea about yourself, other people, society, or your environment. From birth until death, you are constantly building, altering, and shaping your core beliefs. But they are initially established by your earliest memories—and, given the brain's preference for storing negative events over positive ones, those memories are typically filled with uncomfortable emotions and negative thoughts drawn from how your parents raised you. If the painful experiences you had as a child are never properly dealt with (e.g., trauma treatment by a mental health therapist), the core beliefs created from these memories will continue to skew the way you view yourself.

In chapter 6, I'll go into more detail on outward-facing core beliefs (beliefs you have about other people, the world, and the future), but for now let's focus on inward-facing core beliefs—the beliefs you have about yourself. Core beliefs related to the self can be classified into one of four groups: control, safety, worthiness, and shame:

- Lack of control beliefs often sound like "I am powerless," "I have no control," or "I can't handle parenting."

- Lack of safety beliefs may include thoughts like "I'm unsafe," "I can't keep myself protected," or "I'll get hurt."

- Beliefs related to being unworthy may consist of "I'm not capable," "I'm not good enough," or "I'm defective."

- Shame about who you are can lead to core beliefs like "I'm a horrible parent because of the choices I made," "I can't change," or "I shouldn't be here."

Many parents with these inward-facing core beliefs will perceive their child's behavior as a reflection of themselves. For example, Tony started bringing his son, Paul, to see me when he got caught ditching school. Tony had enacted strong consequences in response to Paul's behavior because it triggered his core belief that he was powerless and unworthy of respect. Rather than viewing Paul's behavior as a reflection of Paul's desires and feelings, Tony viewed it as a reflection of the beliefs he secretly held about himself.

Once core beliefs such as these are formed, you become more aware of experiences, feelings, and emotions that support that belief. Each time an event occurs that reminds you of your core belief, that belief is strengthened, resulting in a cycle of negative thinking from which it is hard to break free.

The Cycle of Negative Thinking

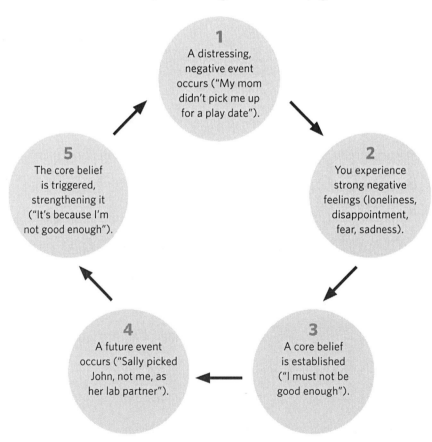

1
A distressing, negative event occurs ("My mom didn't pick me up for a play date").

2
You experience strong negative feelings (loneliness, disappointment, fear, sadness).

3
A core belief is established ("I must not be good enough").

4
A future event occurs ("Sally picked John, not me, as her lab partner").

5
The core belief is triggered, strengthening it ("It's because I'm not good enough").

Once you get caught in this circular process, you come to view the world through the distorted lens of this core belief. You tend to assume that other people's actions say something negative about you, even when they don't. For example, Clare shared in one session that her son had told her he wasn't dating anyone, but later she learned that he had been hanging out with a girl from school. "I feel like I'm trash when I'm lied to about dumb things," Clare lamented. There was no evidence to suggest that Clare's son was behaving this way because he viewed her as "trash." In fact, there were several alternative (and more likely) reasons for his behavior. For example, he may genuinely view this girl as just a friend, or he may define dating differently from how his mother defines it.

Why didn't Clare consider these alternative explanations? Because the quickest and easiest way for the brain to interpret the world is through the lens of the preexisting core beliefs (regardless of how inaccurate they may be). In essence, your brain lies to you by telling you what you already believe. This process is facilitated by a vital part of your brain called the reticular activating system (RAS). Your brain doesn't have the ability to process everything your senses perceive. If it did, you would likely shut down from the overwhelming amount of information coming in—the myriad of things that you can see, hear, taste, and touch at any given moment. Your RAS filters this sensory information, selecting which pieces of data to pass on to other parts of your brain.

Unfortunately, the RAS tends to focus on the details your brain is already familiar with. It's like a nightclub bouncer, letting in the details that are already on the list but stopping unfamiliar data, including those that might be up-and-comers. As a result, the core beliefs you established in childhood are reaffirmed when new challenging, painful, confusing, or negative information comes in. This not only causes you pain and heartache but will also influence how you interpret your child's actions. Unless your negative core beliefs are properly identified, challenged, and altered, they will continue to be strengthened throughout your life.

It's important to note two more things: first, that most parents are unaware of their core beliefs, and second, that these negative core beliefs are often not true. Like Clare, your perception of your child's actions and feelings may not be accurate. That's why it's essential to start identifying what you think about yourself and how your brain has been explaining certain events that have happened to you.

Activity 1.1
Identifying Inward-Facing Core Beliefs

This activity will help you explore what your brain has been telling you. In the space provided, write down the core beliefs you have about yourself. Your core beliefs should be written in the form of a descriptive "I" statement rather than an interpretive statement. For example, *My mother didn't think I was good enough* isn't a core belief; it's an explanation of how you interpreted your mother's actions. *I am not good enough* is a statement that describes why you believe certain things have happened to you. As painful as this activity may be, it will be immensely helpful in learning to see your child's behavior for what it is, not how it looks through the lens of your own childhood pain.

Your Core Beliefs Reveal Your Unmet Core Needs

The most effective way to alter your negative core beliefs is to meet your unmet needs from childhood. Core needs are human requirements for safety, comfort, and belonging that must be met for optimum psychological, physical, and emotional development. Although people articulate their core needs differently, every negative core belief you have will reveal what needs you are currently lacking.

For example, Clare's core needs—in her words, "to be loved, accepted, wanted, and worthy"—were primarily caused by her belief that she wasn't wanted by her mother. Similarly, you may have experienced events in childhood where your needs weren't met (e.g., a parent forgetting your soccer tournament), which left you feeling unimportant, forgotten, or not cared for. These feelings then caused your brain to create a negative core belief.

Now you may be thinking, *But Dr. Brie, my past wasn't that bad!* or *My parents did the best they could, and I love them.* I absolutely believe you and your perspective on your childhood. But even if your parents were wonderful or you had a pretty good childhood, you can still grow up with unresolved feelings and unmet needs. In other words, both things can be true! Regardless of how you would describe your childhood (e.g., challenging, traumatic, healthy, terrific), if you are dismissing or minimizing emotions, or avoiding reflecting on your past, there is healing that needs to take place to help you stop parenting through the past.

Therefore, it is important to closely examine your core beliefs and core needs if you want to stop parenting the child you were. In fact, until you do, you will continue trying to get your core needs met through your child.

Before you start feeling guilt and shame for parenting in this way, let me assure you that this is an incredibly common experience for parents. Your brain desperately wants to change your core beliefs for the better, but it can only do that if your core needs are met. Once you learn how to meet your needs, it will alter your parenting styles that aren't working for your child.

Activity 1.2
Identifying Unmet Needs

This activity will help you identify which core needs were not met during your childhood. Read through the descriptions of the different types of core needs, and write down any unmet needs you have within each category. If you aren't sure how to categorize a particular need, choose whatever instinctively feels right. Writing down and acknowledging the core need is more important than making sure it goes in the "correct" spot, and many needs overlap in different categories (for example, *I wasn't heard* may fall into both emotional and psychological safety).

Physical safety, comfort, and belonging: Physical needs involve experiencing a safe living environment free from abuse and neglect. Examples of physical needs include, but are not limited to, a stable place to live, clean water, medical attention when necessary, and feeling safe around family members and other people in your home.

_____

_____

_____

_____

_____

_____

Emotional safety, comfort, and belonging: Emotional needs deal with feelings of respect, importance, emotional security, inclusion, and acceptance. For example, one emotional need is the ability to voice your feelings and thoughts to your primary caregivers and having them acknowledge your experiences. Examples of unmet needs include *I wasn't wanted, I didn't belong anywhere,* and *I wasn't comforted when I was sad.*

_____

_____

_____

_____

_____

_____

Psychological safety, comfort, and belonging: Psychological needs involve a healthy balance of autonomy and connection—feeling accepted for who you are and empowered to become who you want to be. Unmet needs can include not being sure of how your parent will react to an accident (will they understand, or will they scream at you?), low self-esteem and self-worth (not feeling capable of achieving something), or inappropriate independence (such as walking home because a parent forgot to pick you up).

_____

_____

_____

_____

_____

_____

Chapter 2

How to Identify If You're Parenting Through Your Past

The concept of "parenting through the past" can seem abstract and vague. To better understand this parenting style, it's useful to recognize how it shows up in the thoughts, phrases, and actions that parents commonly express. If any of the examples in this chapter sound familiar, don't worry—you haven't permanently damaged your child or your relationship with them. Recognizing the personal behaviors you would like to change is the crucial first step in building a better relationship with your child. So instead of beating yourself up, I encourage you to grab a pen and a journal and make notes of the patterns you see in yourself. It can also be helpful to ask a trusted person close to you, such as your spouse or therapist, to identify behaviors they see you practicing. If you start to feel triggered or overwhelmed, it's okay to take a break and come back to the list later.

Knee-Jerk Reactions

Think back to the last time you were in the heat of an argument with your child. Did you make a comment or take an action that you immediately regretted? Every parent I've worked with has admitted to having knee-jerk responses sometimes. There's a part of the brain, called the amygdala, that becomes activated when it senses that your safety is at risk. Your amygdala will try to help you feel safe and in control again, using one of the three methods it knows: fighting, fleeing, or freezing. But while this mechanism is a great asset in the face of sudden danger (like being attacked by a grizzly bear), the amygdala also tends to go off when there's no immediate danger and you're simply feeling angry or fearful. This can result in knee-jerk reactions when you encounter criticism or judgment, when you feel unsafe, or when you attempt to shield your child from challenges similar to what you faced when growing up.

Criticism and Judgment

Danny was shopping in the grocery store with his daughter, Lizzy, when she asked him to buy her favorite fruit snacks. When Danny said no, she began crying loudly and making a scene. Feeling judged by the stares of other shoppers, Danny gave in, throwing the box into the cart. But while this response made Lizzy stop crying, it didn't take away Danny's feeling of being judged. "I don't want people thinking I'm a bad parent," he admitted to me.

Like Danny, you may be familiar with the feeling of being judged for your child's behavior. It may be catching looks from strangers, overhearing comments from friends, or receiving criticism from family members about your child and how you're raising them. Regardless of where it comes from, judgment can trigger the negative core beliefs created by the unmet needs of your childhood. Knee-jerk reactions are your brain's attempt to quickly combat the uncomfortable feelings that those core beliefs bring up.

Even though Danny knew giving his daughter the fruit snacks would only encourage her to behave the same way the next time they were in the store, the perceived criticism triggered his fear of not being a good enough parent, leading him to make an impulsive decision that he'd regret later. When I asked Danny about times when he didn't feel good enough as a child, he mentioned an occasion when he was the only kid not invited to a party in junior high school. For him, that experience had translated into a core belief—"I was not good enough for them to even invite me"—that had been strengthened by other experiences throughout his life. Decades later, Danny shared that he still deeply longs to be told by someone that he is good enough.

Lack of Safety

Molly was playing cars with her two-year-old son, Gino, when out of nowhere, he reached up and slapped her so hard that the glasses flew off her face. "Next thing I knew," Molly confessed, "I was hitting him back. I can't believe I would hit my own child. It's like I had zero control of my body or thoughts." Afterward, Gino flinched anytime she got near him. For Molly, there was only one awful conclusion to draw: "I'm a horrible mother."

The human brain is wired to seek physical safety before it considers anything else. If you perceive an immediate threat, like someone running after you holding a knife, your mind doesn't pause to wonder about the reason for it; it immediately triggers your body to start running. Similarly, the shock of being hit, kicked, slapped, or bitten, even if it's by your own child, makes it hard not to respond impulsively. Your self-protective reaction can happen so quickly that you don't have a chance to respond the way you'd like to.

To help Molly process the event with her son, I asked her about other times she felt unsafe in her life. She shared that she grew up with an older brother who physically threatened and abused her when her parents weren't home. Moreover, because she couldn't stand the thought of raising a son who would hurt someone like her brother had hurt her, Molly admitted that she spanked Gino when he showed aggression toward others. Even though Molly knew her two-year-old lacked an adult's ability to appropriately express his anger, her fears were triggered by her unmet childhood need for physical safety.

Attempting to Avoid Similar Challenges

Finally, knee-jerk reactions can reflect an effort to prevent your child from experiencing the same pain or challenges you endured as a child. I don't blame any parent for wanting to protect their child from the worst emotions and events they can imagine. But if you're responding to your child based on your past, you likely aren't accurately perceiving what they need in the present.

For example, Sam and her husband caught their daughter, Lily, in the act of sneaking out of the house after curfew to be with her boyfriend. This was a direct violation of the rules they'd set, and they responded by grounding Lily for three months. "That might seem harsh to you," Sam told me, "but I was reckless as a teenager, and I refuse to let my daughter make similar mistakes."

I learned that Sam gave birth to Lily when she was seventeen and that she struggled for years after that to give her daughter a good life. Constantly on alert for the risk of her daughter becoming a teen mom, Sam found it difficult to remain calm when Lily engaged in undesirable behaviors. "I didn't work this hard for her to follow in my footsteps," she professed.

Rarely does a knee-jerk reaction prove to be the best decision. Although the previous examples may not seem deeply inappropriate or likely to cause lifelong harm, they're not the decisions these parents would have made if they were able to self-soothe, set their own trauma aside, and identify what their child really needed in those moments. It can be very difficult to regulate your emotions and make a logical decision in the midst of a triggering situation, but slowing down to consider other information and your child's needs is crucial to prevent you from parenting through the past.

Living Vicariously Through Your Child

Another common pattern I see in those who parent through the past is that they live vicariously through their children. While many people wish they could change various aspects of their childhood, from the sports they participated in to the academic opportunities they had (or lacked), some parents go one step further by giving their child the experiences they wish they'd had, regardless of whether their child even wants them.

Giving Your Child What You Didn't Have

Javier was raised by a single father who worked constantly just to keep food on the table. Because his family didn't have extra money for him to do things like play sports or join clubs, Javier was determined to give his own children those opportunities, no matter what. "My wife and I have definitely gotten into fights about money," Javier admitted to me. "She wants them to earn money and learn responsibility, but I want them to enjoy their lives and not worry about money. I refuse to not spend money on my kids. I can't imagine telling them, 'No, we don't have the money for that.'"

It's neither abnormal nor bad to want to give your children a better life than you had. However, being unable to consider current information (such as your spouse's opinion) when making parenting decisions is a clear sign that you're parenting the child you were, not the child you have.

Acceptance from Others

"I think Olivia would love being a cheerleader if she just gave it a shot," Alex told me. "School would be so much more enjoyable for her, and she'd automatically be in the popular crowd. That's why I've made her continue gymnastics. I can't wait to cheer her on at games and watch her have the best time in high school."

Once children enter the teen years, parents often begin attempting to redo their own adolescence by pressuring their child to engage in the activities they wish they had experienced in school. Alex admitted to wanting to be a cheerleader when she was younger but insisted she was only forcing her daughter into it because it would help her make friends. Motivated by her own unmet need of belonging in childhood, Alex planned outings to cheer events and paid for her daughter to learn tumbling skills rather than encouraging her to find clubs and sports that she wanted to participate in.

Avoiding Labels

While taking her son Theo out to dinner with one of his friends, Melanie became bothered by Theo's unusual behavior—"bouncing off the walls," as she put it—and admonished him for it. In recounting the story, she explained, "I pulled Theo aside and told him, 'You're being too much.' I was so bothered by his behavior, and I didn't want other people calling him names or judging him. People constantly told me I was 'too much' and I didn't want him to be perceived the same way."

Harsh labels given to children often stick with them for years, so it's hardly surprising that parents who grew up with labels like *needy*, *weird, stupid,* or *difficult* don't want their children to go through the same humiliation. However, sometimes these parents force their children to engage in certain behaviors, activities, or experiences in the hope that it will help them avoid those labels and thereby satisfy the parent's unmet need. Paradoxically, the parent might even criticize their child in an attempt to spare them from criticism, as Melanie did when she placed the label of "too much" onto Theo.

"I Do the Opposite of What My Parents Did"

From being harshly punished for minor infractions to having super strict rules for their behavior, some parents absolutely hated how they were raised, leading them to make a conscious decision to parent in the opposite way. While it's understandable that they would want to break a harmful pattern, especially one that involved abuse or neglect, taking a "do the opposite" approach often shows up as parenting from a place of painful resentment or a desire to prove their own parent wrong.

Explaining Everything

Whenever Candace's six-year-old daughter, Leah, questions one of her rules or parenting decisions, Candace makes it a point to explain her reasoning in detail. "I didn't like being told 'because I said so' when I was growing up, so I explain everything to my kid. I'm not trying to justify my parenting choices, but if Leah doesn't like a choice I'm making, she knows she's allowed to try to change my mind," Candace told me.

Many of today's parents were raised with the "children should be seen, not heard" philosophy of previous generations and, as a result, have swayed to the opposite end of the spectrum by allowing their children to have a voice in every decision. While it's commendable to want your child to feel like their opinion matters, constantly explaining your reasoning can cause children to struggle with boundaries in other areas of life. For instance, Leah often pushed back when her teacher gave her homework.

By raising her daughter in the opposite way of how her parents raised her, Candace hoped to help Leah avoid the uncomfortable emotions she had as a child. She explained to me, "I wanted to feel like an equal when I was a child, and I don't want my daughter feeling like her opinions don't matter." However, this effort was preventing Candace from seeing her daughter's actual needs.

Idle or Helicopter Parenting

Earlier generations often raised their children with too much attention ("helicopter" parents who monitored everything their child did) or too little attention ("idle" parents who were rarely around). Either extreme can cause the next generation to parent in the exact opposite manner. Whether you wish your parents had been more laid back or more attentive, the important point is that this is the parenting style *you* wanted, not necessarily the one your child currently needs to thrive and grow.

For example, Owen and Elena came to therapy for help with their sixteen-year-old son's habit of drinking and using vape pens. Elena was concerned that their son was heading down the wrong path and needed rules. Owen, however, believed it was just typical teen behavior. When Elena would give their son a curfew, Owen would tell him not to worry about it and enjoy his night.

During treatment, it became clear that Owen's parenting style was related to his own upbringing as an adopted child, where he was constantly under a microscope. "I had so many rules as a kid, and it was awful! Kids need freedom to learn and grow. I don't think they should be smothered and constantly told what to do." Owen's idea of freedom, dictated by his own lack of independence as a teenager, meant letting his son come and go as he pleased, with no boundaries or consequences for his behavior.

Overly Structured Parenting

People who grew up without a lot of discipline tend to resent their parents for not teaching or supervising them more, believing that more structure would have helped them become better people. These individuals can hold lingering resentment that prevents them from seeing their own children's needs, leading them to assume a more authoritarian role in parenting. As a result, their children can feel unseen and may even come to believe that their parents don't trust them.

For example, having grown up without a father figure in his life, Charles was a firm believer that kids need discipline and structure to become successful adults. "My mom didn't have the time or energy to parent me the way I should have been parented," Charles told me. "If I'd had the structure I provide to my children, I can only imagine the type of person I would have become. I will be everything my deadbeat dad wasn't."

Charles struggled for years with pain and heartache due to his father abandoning him. "He would call twice a year and tell me he would come pick me up, but he would never show," Charles remembered. "I rebelled and put my mom through hell. When I married my wife, I vowed to be the disciplinarian father I needed." Charles believed that by creating an enormous amount of structure and rules for his children, he was helping them avoid life challenges. In reality, he was attempting to get his needs met by becoming the father he wanted as a child.

"This Worked for Me as a Kid"

Just as parenting in the exact opposite way from your parents is a lose-lose situation for you and your child, so is intentionally raising your child identically to how you were parented. If one parenting method worked for every person on the planet, parenting books (and family therapists like me) wouldn't exist. Parents who don't take the time to learn new ways of communicating or connecting with their children are ignoring the fact that every child is unique and thus needs different parenting methods to thrive. However, if you ask these parents about the reason behind their methods, they will respond, "That's how I was raised, and I turned out just fine."

Insults and Name-Calling

Dev grew up with parents who would call him lazy and tell him he couldn't achieve his goals. "That totally helped motivate me," Dev insisted. "I remember thinking to myself, *I'm going to prove them wrong*, and I did!" Because Dev credits his successful career to his parents straightening him up as a teen, he can't understand why the same approach doesn't work for his son.

Like Dev, many parents attempt to use reverse psychology (as they understand it) to motivate their children. Even if this approach happened to work for you growing up, don't expect it to work for your child. In general, people do not respond well to insults, name-calling, or being told they can't do something, and for children, this can be particularly offensive and hurtful.

When Dev's son began struggling with doing homework, as many teenagers do, Dev started admonishing him, "Don't be lazy!" While Dev thought this insult didn't seem to faze his son, he learned during therapy that his son had actually come to hate him because of it.

Thanks to the name-calling, his son's self-worth was dropping along with his grades.

Enmeshed Closeness

Growing up, Meredith loved the closeness she had with her mother; their "best friend" relationship validated Meredith's sense of identity and self-worth. "I want to be able to do this for Harper," she explained to me, adding, "I love being the 'cool mom' and hearing Harper's friends tell her they wish their moms were like me."

Meredith's husband saw the overly close relationship she had with their daughter as a lack of boundaries, and he pointed out how Meredith would tell Harper things that she didn't even tell him. "My husband doesn't understand what it was like for me to grow up with only my mom," Meredith argued. "We really grew up together. She told me everything, and being there for her made me who I am. I want Harper to have the same relationship with me."

Many people who were extremely close to their parents believe that it's the reason they grew up to be successful, happy, or productive people. Even though this isn't necessarily a negative parenting style, it can block you from identifying the specific needs your child has, leading to an overly enmeshed relationship that negatively impacts your child's individual growth and development. For Harper, the lack of boundaries caused her to view herself as her parents' peer rather than as a child. She flouted their rules, neglecting her chores and schoolwork and staying out past curfew.

Lawnmower Parents

Parents who experienced difficulty as children often attempt to prevent their own children from experiencing similar heartache by pushing all obstacles out of the child's way. These "lawnmower" parents, as I call them, became a major news topic after the 2019 college admissions scandal, when a number of parents were caught falsifying applications and bribing college officials to get their children admitted to top universities. That story is an extreme example of parents who will do everything in their power to create a life of ease and effortless opportunity for their children.

Removing Work

Joe's family struggled financially throughout his childhood, to the point that they couldn't afford to send him to college. Joe couldn't fathom putting his daughter through the same experience, so rather than ask her to work part-time in high school to help save for college, he took out loans to pay for her education without discussing it with his wife. "I want my daughter to have the best life imaginable," he insisted. "If my wife and I need to take a second mortgage out to pay for her to go to the best college, I'll do it."

Parents who can't handle watching their children struggle to earn or learn something may proactively remove obstacles for them, which teaches the children to expect that things will be handed to them. This is where we get the theory that money skips a generation: When parents who struggled to make a good living give their children everything, those children end up unable to provide for themselves because important lessons were removed from their lives.

Fearing Similar Outcomes

Penny and her husband could not agree on how to handle their daughter's depression and lack of motivation. Penny's tactic had been to remove chores, consequences, and responsibilities. "I think it's my job to make life easier for her right now, not harder!" she explained. Penny shared in therapy that her brother died by suicide when they were both young. "When my daughter tells me she's depressed, why would I give her more responsibility?" she reasoned, fearful that doing so would lead to her daughter feeling overwhelmed and shutting down or harming herself.

Parents who have lost a loved one or witnessed someone close to them endure a terrible challenge are often fearful of losing their child in a similar way. However, this fear can cause them to miss their child's real needs. Penny's constant enabling only encouraged her daughter to sink deeper into a state of helpless dependence, increasing both parents' frustration with her and with each other. Ultimately, life in their home became so fraught that Penny and her husband ended up getting divorced.

Fixing Everything

Theresa felt frustrated by her daughter Becky's expectation that Theresa help her get ready for prom. "I gave her my credit card to go to the salon and get her hair and nails done with her friends," Theresa complained, "but it's still not enough for her. She asked why I don't want to spend the time with her. It has nothing to do with that—of course I want to spend time with her, but I don't know how to do her hair or nails. It'll look better if someone else does them."

A common feature of lawnmower parenting is seeing the child's needs as obstacles that require a specific "fix." Often, this leads to frustration when the parent feels unqualified to provide that help. However, when your child brings problems or difficult situations to you, all they really want is to connect with you, not to have you fix the situation for them. Because Theresa viewed Becky's need to get ready for prom as an obstacle that she could most effectively fix with money, she did not notice Becky's real need for time and emotional connection with her mother.

Removing challenges from your child's way in an effort to avoid pain, heartache, or difficulty won't give your child an easier life; it will actually cause the exact opposite. When children have opportunities to persevere through challenges, they learn valuable life lessons that increase their self-worth and help prepare them for their adult lives. The next activity will help you identify which of the parenting styles you commonly use and why.

Activity 2.1
Your Go-To Method

It is completely normal to use parenting methods you aren't proud of, but in order to start changing them, you must first acknowledge them. As you read about the parenting styles in this chapter, you may have already identified one or two you commonly use. If not, take some time to think about a recent interaction you had with your child, and select the parenting style it most closely resembles.

Which parenting style were you using?

- ☐ Knee-jerk reaction
- ☐ Living vicariously through your child
- ☐ Parenting the opposite of your parents
- ☐ Parenting the same as your parents
- ☐ Removing obstacles for your child

Write what you remember about this interaction. What did you feel and think in the moment? What was your goal when using this parenting method (e.g., seeking compliance, trying to control your child, hoping to feel good enough)?

_____

_____

_____

_____

_____

What Difference Does It Make to You?

After I take parents through the different styles of parenting through the past, their first response is usually something like this: "But you don't understand—I'm doing this *for my child.*" I don't doubt their sincerity; most parents are genuinely trying to do the best job they can. The problem is that parenting through your past is a subconscious choice based on emotion, rather than a conscious choice based on knowledge and reason.

When you are parenting through your past, you are making decisions based on your own unhealed trauma or childhood pain, which prevents the emotional and logical hemispheres of your brain from communicating with each other. While the logical side of your brain is trying to raise your child in the way you believe is right and reasonable, the emotional side of your brain is screaming, "If I don't do these things, I will have failed as a parent!" Even the "right" parenting decision can yield the "wrong" result if it's motivated by the chaotic emotions that accompany unhealed trauma.

To help the logical side of the brain catch up with the emotional side, I ask every parent one specific question that identifies whose need—yours or your child's—is being met in any given parenting scenario. I typically have to pose this question four to six times before the root answer is finally revealed. Here's the question:

What difference would it make to you
if your ideal outcome occurred?

For a clear example, let's return to one of the cases described earlier. Make sure you pay attention to the "difference" question and how the parent responds.

Getting to the Root

During one therapy session, Candace described a recent tantrum that happened after Leah asked for two cookies. Candace responded, "No, it's almost time for dinner. I want to make sure you eat healthy and get plenty of nutrients, and cookies will spoil your dinner."

Leah argued, "Well, you need nutrients, too, and *you* get to eat cookies. I also plan on eating cookies after dinner, so it doesn't matter which one comes first."

Candace admitted to feeling irritated with Leah for not accepting her decision. While she wanted her daughter to have a voice, she felt burned out from constantly giving explanations.

This is where the "difference" question came in.

Dr. Brie: Candace, you've raised a very articulate, determined little girl. To understand her tantrums a bit more, I'm curious about the explanations you give to Leah. Can you tell me more about them?

Candace: I think it's important for her to hear my explanation. [*Note: This is the desired outcome—the first one, anyway.*] Sometimes she will come up with really good reasons why she should get to do something, and I'll let her.

Dr. Brie: Wow. That's impressive for six years old. I'm curious where your desire to give her an explanation came from.

Candace: When I was a kid, I hated being told "Because I said so" by my mother. So, Dave and I decided we would never say that to our kids. We want them to have a voice and opinion when we make choices.

Dr. Brie: This might be a strange question, but—if Leah is able to hear your explanations, what difference would that make for you? [*This is the first time I ask the "difference" question*].

Candace: Oh, um . . . I think Leah will be able to grow up and articulate what she wants and needs. [*Notice that a new desired outcome has been identified.*]

Dr. Brie: Okay, great! And if Leah is able to articulate her wants and needs, what difference would that make for *you*? [*This is the second time I've asked her the "difference" question.*]

Candace: I think she'd be independent and not have to rely on people to make decisions for her, like I did. [*Yet another desired outcome.*] I was always told what to do and never allowed to think for myself.

Dr. Brie: That must have been hard for you. If Leah grows up to be independent, what difference would that make for *you*? [*Third time.*]

Candace: Well, I guess I would think that I did a good job [*another desired outcome*]—a better job than my parents, for sure— because I raised a child who can think for herself.

Dr. Brie: And if you did a good job raising her, what difference would that make for you? [*Fourth time.*]

Candace: That I'm a good mom. [*At last, we've arrived at the root desired outcome.*]

Dr. Brie: That makes a lot of sense to me. I'm curious if you felt good enough when you were a child?

As you can see, it took Candace four tries to dig deep enough to identify the difference her desired outcomes would have for *her*, not her child. I stopped asking when her answer finally focused on herself and revealed a core need: the psychological need to feel like a good mom.

Activity 2.2
What Difference Does It Make?

Review your answers from activity 2.1—in particular, the parenting style you used or the choice you made, and the behavior from your child that you wanted to see result from it. For example, maybe you recently emailed your child's math teacher to say that your child's homework would be late due to a sports game. The desired result might have been to ensure your child gets a good night's rest and doesn't have to worry about the math assignment.

Parenting choice: _____

_____

_____

_____

Desired result: _____

_____

_____

_____

As you reflect on the choice and desired result, what difference would it make to *you* if the desired result happened?

_____

_____

_____

_____

Look at the answer you just wrote down and ask yourself again: What difference would it make to *you* if that desired result happened?

Look at the answer you just wrote down and ask yourself again: What difference would it make to *you* if that desired result happened?

Look at the answer you just wrote down and ask yourself again: What difference would it make to *you* if that desired result happened?

Continue to ask yourself that question until you find an answer that (1) focuses on you and not your child and (2) identifies a core unmet need. This may or may not surprise you, but your final root answer to this question will likely bear a close resemblance to an answer you gave when identifying your unmet childhood needs in activity 1.2.

The Worst Is Over

The most important aspect of parenting is accurately identifying and meeting your child's needs. The choices you make when you're parenting through the past might not seem deeply inappropriate or harmful, but they're not the decisions you would have made if you could have identified what your child really needed in those moments. Although it can be very difficult when you're in the midst of a triggering situation, slowing down to consider other information and your child's authentic needs is crucial.

Remember, it's completely normal to use parenting methods you aren't proud of. But you must acknowledge these tendencies so that you can begin changing them. It's not easy to face your parenting missteps, focus on whose needs are being met in these instances, and dig deep into your unmet needs and core beliefs. The good news is that you've already made it through some of the most challenging information I ask parents to work through. You should be proud of your honesty, bravery, and strength. By reflecting on your past, you're on your way to altering decades of negative family patterns that hurt the child you used to be—and one step closer to raising and bonding with the child you have.

Part 2

—

Parenting Through Your Past Is Harming Your Present

Chapter 3

How Parenting Through Your Past Impacts Your Child, Your Family, and You

I receive phone calls on a daily basis from parents who are desperate to change their child's behavior. The first thing I have to tell them is probably the last thing they want to hear: I can't make their child change. The bright side, however, is that I can help the parents change how they are parenting, which will pave the way for significant improvements in their relationship with their child.

Believe it or not, the parent-child relationship is more important than the behaviors you want to change. Even "problem children" can grow up into healthy, high-functioning adults if their foundational needs for safety, love, and security are met. But without those needs being met, good behavior is just a ticking time bomb. While your child's tantrums or rebellion may seem bad now, their impact will be much worse when those unmet needs manifest in adulthood.

This chapter explores the short- and long-term consequences of parenting through the past. I review how this parenting style can cause several major problems in your child's life, all of which lead to the undesirable behaviors you are seeking to change. In addition, I discuss the impact of parenting through your past on other relationships within the family unit, including sibling relationships, the relationship you have with your spouse or partner, and even the relationship you have with yourself.

How Parenting Through Your Past Impacts Your Child

Your Child's Needs Aren't Met

As you learned in chapter 1, parenting through your past makes it extremely difficult to meet your child's needs because your brain is occupied with fulfilling your own unmet needs from childhood. In other words, without knowing it, you're putting your needs above your child's, leaving them to try to fulfill their needs somewhere else. Screaming toddlers, physically aggressive tweens, and sexual-risk-taking teenagers all have one thing in common: They have a need that isn't being recognized and met. If there is only one thing you take away from this book, let it be that unmet needs can cause undesirable behaviors, often in the form of acting out or emotional explosions.

Acting Out

Seven-year-old Luis was brought to therapy due to his pattern of hitting, kicking, and pushing his parents and siblings. During a play therapy activity, Luis shared with me that he was worried about dying. When he was three, he experienced a severe medical trauma that led to numerous hospital visits. Even though he was very young, he remembered feeling alone and afraid that he would die.

I asked Luis to tell me about the last time he felt alone. "Yesterday," he answered, "when my brother wouldn't play with me." When I asked what he did when he felt alone like that, Luis said he would hit and kick, trying to get someone to play with him. He added that his parents would discipline him with a time-out in his room, and that made him feel even more alone.

When a child's needs go unmet—whether it's because of a traumatic event or being parented through the past—their little body and brain remember that incident and the terrible feeling it caused. From that time forward, that need is triggered anytime they believe the same feeling could occur.

In response to these triggers, it's common for young children to act out in the form of tantrums, aggression, or bad attitudes. As children age, most stop showing aggression, but they will start acting out in other ways to get their needs met. Teenagers hoping to feel loved by or good enough for someone may engage in risky sexual behaviors or become fixated on having a partner. Or, hoping to fit in with others, they may use recreational drugs or alcohol. In recent years, online gaming and social media have also become common venues for adolescents to fulfill their needs or at least numb their uncomfortable feelings.

Acting out doesn't end when the child reaches adulthood. For example, Lauren grew up with the knowledge that her parents had dropped out of college after becoming pregnant with her. They paid for her college education with the expectation that she would earn a civil engineering degree and complete the career path they had abandoned. With so much pressure to fulfill her parents' dreams, Lauren turned to alcohol and drugs to numb her feelings.

Emotional Explosions

Ten-year-old Nevaeh struggled with a pattern of explosive tantrums and chronic panic attacks that only happened around her mother, Jasmine. To reduce her daughter's anxiety, Jasmine would try to reassure her by saying, "Everything is fine" and "You're okay." But rather than calm her down, this made Nevaeh feel like her mom wasn't listening to her, which triggered anger and panic attacks on top of the anxiety.

Along with a limited vocabulary, children have limited insight as to why they are upset. Their brain is only able to tell them, *You aren't safe/wanted/loved/good enough.* When these thoughts occur, the child tries to prove those beliefs wrong by dominating a situation with "noisy" emotions like anger, sadness, anxiety, and hostility.

When asked about their family dynamics, Jasmine shared that her biggest fear was that Nevaeh would grow up to be just like her—anxious and unhappy. How ironic that Jasmine's fear of her daughter becoming an unhappy person was actually causing the explosive emotions she wanted to change.

Your Child Doesn't Get to Have Their Own Experiences

Even though acting-out behaviors and emotional explosions are the primary reasons parents seek therapy, there is an even bigger consequence that occurs when you parent through your past: Your child doesn't get to live their own life. Whether your parenting choices reflect an attempt to get your own needs met or to help your child avoid difficult challenges, parenting from your past removes opportunities for your child to develop resilience, character, and stamina. These children may grow into adults who struggle with decision-making, problem-solving, and self-regulation.

Decision-Making and Problem-Solving

Childhood, especially the teen years, is a time for individuals to start experimenting with who they are—everything from hobbies and interests to morals, values, goals, and dreams. Making their own decisions, including decisions that turn out to be mistakes, is an important part of this experimentation. Adjusting to and managing the consequences of unwanted results is a child's primary means of learning about themselves and how they can meet their own needs.

Many adults who weren't given the chance as children to experiment and problem-solve struggle to confront challenges in later years. When presented with difficult events in adulthood, they fall victim to paralysis by analysis. For example, Tom shared that when he was growing up, his father, a prominent figure in their community, threw his weight around to get Tom involved in high school sports teams and community groups that would enhance his college applications. But because Tom's confidence and independence were never established as a child, college proved to be overwhelming for him; he was always fearful of making the wrong choice. As he put it, "I'm so afraid to make the wrong decision that I won't make one. I go with the flow and let others make decisions."

On the other end of the spectrum, children who were not taught to delay gratification while analyzing potential options may become impulsive decision-makers as adults. When a choice is presented to them, they choose the option that seems to immediately fulfill their needs, at least in the short term. One thirty-year-old client shared, "I struggle to keep a relationship going because when I feel like the person isn't making me happy anymore, I just leave and find another person."

Self-Regulation

Layla grew up with a mother whose extreme emotions made it hard for Layla to feel any of her own. Ever since, she has struggled to understand or even identify what she's feeling. "I don't know whether I'm scared, nervous, lonely . . . anything," Layla said. "And because I don't know what I'm feeling, I don't know how to fix it." As an adult, Layla has had to work on developing skills she should have learned in childhood, such as naming her emotions and self-soothing in moments of emotional overwhelm.

Children are born unable to self-regulate (or self-soothe), which is why they cry out for a parent to meet their need (feed them, change them, comfort them). This gives the child an example of how to self-regulate until they eventually learn techniques for soothing their own emotions and choosing appropriate behaviors in the face of triggering events or overwhelm. This learning by example is known as co-regulation.

Unfortunately, a parent with unmet needs will not only struggle to self-regulate but also be unable to co-regulate with their child. If you've ever gone to soothe a crying baby while you were agitated or upset, there's a good chance the baby didn't respond to your efforts. Even at a young age, children can sense your distress and follow your behavior. They will conclude that you're unable to understand and meet their need. My adult clients whose parents were unable to self-regulate describe their own experiences similarly to Layla:

"I don't know how to calm down when I'm upset."

"When I'm upset, I either avoid thinking about it or cry myself to sleep."

"I was put in time-out or spanked when I was a kid. Now I just think that when I show an emotion, someone will get mad at me."

> Think about a time you witnessed your parent experiencing a
> distressing emotion (e.g., anger, sadness, loneliness) that was
> unrelated to you. What was your response when you saw it? Did you
> attempt to comfort them? Create a more soothing environment?
> Find them someone who could help? You likely attempted to meet
> your parent's need, because deep down you knew that if they
> could not meet their own needs, they could not meet yours.

You Miss Out on Your Child

Finally, one of the saddest effects of parenting through your past is that
it prevents you from learning about who your child is as a person—
their favorite ice cream flavor, their best subjects in school, their
biggest fears, their happiest moments. As a therapist, it always makes
me sad to share things I've learned about a child I'm treating, only to
hear the parents respond, "I had no idea."

With your brain preoccupied by your own needs, you can only
focus on your child as a collection of their observable behaviors,
emotions, and achievements. Knowing their personality is crucial
to being informed about the things that motivate their behaviors,
emotions, and decisions: their worries and fears, their dreams and
aspirations, how they view the world and work through change,
what makes them laugh and cry, their favorite memories and most
embarrassing moments, and most importantly, the ways they
understand and receive love.

Ten years as a therapist has convinced me that everyone's deepest
desire is to be known and understood. But fulfilling this desire for
your child simply isn't possible when your past consistently triggers
your unmet needs to feel safe, accepted, and loved. Addressing your
negative childhood experiences and learning to meet your own needs

opens the door for you to learn who your child really is. The more your child feels seen and understood by you, the fewer emotional and behavioral outbursts you'll see, and the more opportunity you'll have to build the relationship you've longed to have with them.

How Parenting Through Your Past Impacts the Sibling Relationship

Many parents admit to "seeing" themselves in one of their children. This often occurs when a parent and child share the same birth order, gender, interests, or personality traits. Although this isn't necessarily a problem in itself, when a parent has unmet needs from childhood, they may overidentify with this child to the detriment of their relationship with their other children, not to mention the relationships among the siblings. The other children in the family may feel unseen, unheard, disapproved of, or even unwanted, causing them to lash out at the overidentified child. Given that the sibling relationship is typically the longest-lasting relationship people have in their lives, ruptures in this relationship can have enduring effects that people carry with them for years.

To illustrate how these ruptures can manifest, consider the case of Rory and Tiana, who brought their twelve-year-old daughter, Alice, into therapy due to high conflict in the home. Alice, the oldest of their three children, was struggling to get along with her sisters. Tiana described Alice as "incredibly rude" because she never wanted to spend time with her nine-year-old sister, Brit, or include her when Alice's friends came over.

In examining Tiana's own past, I learned that she also had an older sister who teased her and excluded her when she was a child. She explained, "I grew up hating my sister and, to this day, am still really hurt by what she did. I don't want Brit to hate Alice." However, the more Tiana forced Alice to spend time with Brit, the more resentful and angry Alice became toward her parents and siblings. It was clear that due to her own childhood wounds, Tiana was struggling to see Alice's need for healthy independence and was wrongly viewing it as selfish.

How Parenting Through Your Past Impacts Your Relationship with Your Partner

From the moment you began planning to have a child, you likely started thinking about how you would love and nurture that child, including all the ways you would do things better than your parents did. But then your spouse got in the way. (Kidding, of course.) In fact, your spouse or partner likely had their own hopes and visions for how to "do parenting right." Different backgrounds and childhood experiences naturally lead to different parenting philosophies and styles. However, they also lead to different unmet needs, negative core beliefs, and motivations for parenting through the past.

These are the most common concerns I hear from clients who are parenting through their past:

1. They believe their partner is the "problem."

2. They get wrapped up in a parent-focused identity—that is, they only view themselves as a parent, not as a partner or even as an individual.

If you believe your partner is also parenting through their past, I highly recommend you work through this book together and learn how to parent as a team.

Viewing Your Partner as the Problem

When someone is parenting through their past, they often assert that their partner is the reason why their child is struggling. I often hear parents say, "My partner is parenting our child wrong," "My partner is uninvolved (or overly involved)," and "My partner is critical (or a pushover)." In addition to creating conflict with their partner, they may feel overly protective of their child or even inappropriately "team up" with the child against the other parent.

It's important to note that if your child is being physically, emotionally, or psychologically abused by your partner, there is nothing wrong with being overly protective of your child—in fact, it's your job. However, sometimes your past trauma might cause you to inaccurately perceive your partner's behavior as abusive, which triggers you to protect your child rather than evaluate what your child needs.

For example, Derek and Bella brought their fourteen-year-old son, Clark, into therapy for "manipulative behavior" and "playing us off each other." But what started out as an exploration of their son's behavior quickly turned into a discussion of their conflicting parenting styles. At one point, Bella burst into tears, saying, "Derek is so critical of Clark. It's like he purposely doesn't want a relationship with him." Derek defended himself, "I wouldn't be this harsh if she wasn't so soft on him. Anytime I enforce a consequence for Clark's behavior, she undermines me!"

When I asked Bella about her childhood, she explained that her father was severely critical of her and her sister. It made her sad and angry to see what seemed like the same behavior in her husband. For his part, Derek believed the way he was raised was most beneficial: "When I was Clark's age, I had a paper route and mowed lawns. I tell him he's lazy because he doesn't clean up after himself and only plays video games. But Bella is overly attached to Clark and won't teach him responsibilities."

The more Bella protected her son, the harsher Derek became, and vice versa. If Bella or Derek stopped parenting their way, the other parent's style would overcompensate—Clark would either never receive a rule or consequence or receive too many. Along with leaving their son's real needs unmet, parenting through the past had created deep conflict in Bella and Derek's relationship.

Assuming a Parent-Focused Identity

When parents become unintentionally focused on getting their own needs met through their child, their relationship with each other will suffer. Although there is a time and a place to put your child first, especially during their early years or any crisis situations, focusing too heavily on your child's life will cause you to neglect your partner.

For example, Renee brought her sixteen-year-old daughter, Emma, to therapy for help with severe panic attacks. When I asked Renee how she had been responding to Emma thus far, she began to cry, confessing that she struggled to go out with her husband and leave her daughter at home—what would happen if Emma had a panic attack and she wasn't there to help? She had even recently canceled a vacation with her other child just to make sure Emma was okay. Renee's husband, David, shared his frustration toward Renee for spending, in his words, "every waking moment" focused on Emma, to the point that that they hadn't had sex or even been alone in months.

When I asked Renee about her childhood, she shared that she grew up feeling responsible for other people's happiness. The pressure Renee endured as a child caused her to feel overwhelmed by Emma's anxiety with the strong desire to "fix it."

Although it's normal to want to be there for your child when they are in distress, planning your life around the potential discomfort your child *could* experience is a sure way to strain your relationship with your partner. What starts as a decrease in alone time or physical intimacy can lead to a breakdown in communication, an inability to problem-solve or resolve conflict, and eventually serious issues like resentment, name-calling, fights, and even the end of the relationship.

How Parenting Through Your Past Impacts You

The most important relationship you'll ever have in life is with yourself. Therefore, when parents come to me for help with their children's issues, I always recommend that they first take time to reflect on their own unmet needs, core beliefs, and significant life events. As you've already learned, you cannot meet someone else's needs unless yours are met. But the reason goes even deeper than that: In order to have a meaningful relationship with your child, you must first understand and love yourself. As the following examples show, parenting through your past creates a chain reaction that breaks down the relationship you have with yourself by reinforcing your negative core beliefs. In particular, it causes an increase in emotion dysregulation, which then amplifies self-critical thoughts, which results in an inability to heal from the past.

Emotion Dysregulation

If your parenting is an attempt to get your needs met by your child, only one of two outcomes can occur:

- The first possibility is that your child does what you're wanting them to do, causing your needs to be temporarily satisfied. For example, if you clean your child's room every week in order to feel like a good parent, you're likely hoping they will tell you, "Thanks! I love you! You're the best!" While this reaction might feel good in the short term, the long-term consequence is that it reinforces your expectation of getting your needs met by your child in the future. Giving others the power to meet your needs will only cause problems, especially when it's your child. Eventually, your child will give you a response that doesn't satisfy your needs, which will trigger more distressing emotions (frustration, anger, disappointment) than if you hadn't cleaned their room in the first place.

- The second possible outcome is that your child doesn't provide you with the response you are hoping for from the get-go. Chances are, you will experience more frustration, embarrassment, sadness, and irritation because the purpose behind your parenting technique is to meet your own need, not your child's.

For example, Keith's goal was to be the dad he never had. Since Keith's father left him feeling unsupported in his activities and interests, Keith went to the other extreme with his son, Angelo. Not only did he attend Angelo's basketball games, but he also helped him practice and even hired a nutritionist to improve his diet. One day after practice, Keith encouraged Angelo to join him in watching recorded games played by the team he'd be facing next week. But Angelo had plans to spend time with his girlfriend and said he would be home later. Keith's response was to ground Angelo for a week. He also told Angelo that he was an ungrateful son who had no clue how lucky he was. When Keith's need to feel like a better father wasn't met by his son, he lashed out and pushed Angelo away.

When you make other people responsible for meeting your needs, regardless of whether the need is (temporarily) met, you will inevitably feel emotionally dysregulated. In this state of dysregulation, the logical side of your brain goes offline, causing you to be carried into the next link in the chain: self-critical thoughts.

Self-Critical Thoughts

Where emotional dysregulation is present, self-critical thoughts are sure to follow. Once your brain starts on this track, it can be almost impossible to stop and evaluate yourself or your situation accurately. I hear this reflected constantly in the negative self-talk of parents I treat:

"I have no clue what I'm doing."

"I'm turning into my mother (or father)."

"I'm messing up my kids."

For example, when Keith discussed his concerns about his son's lack of motivation and increased defiance, he quickly shifted to self-loathing: "I have no clue where I went wrong. I didn't have a dad who showed up to support me, and now I have a son who is probably better off without me. Should I stop going to his games and give him space?"

As we've discussed already, getting parenting "right" won't heal your childhood traumas or meet your unmet needs. Every parent makes mistakes; dwelling on them will only cause you to believe untrue, unhelpful things about yourself and the job you are doing as a parent. That's why these beliefs trigger the final link in the chain: a perpetuation of the pain of your childhood wounds and a resulting inability to heal from your past.

You Don't Heal

This leads us right back to where we started—to the trauma you endured as a child and the negative core beliefs that it created. Again, trying to prove those beliefs wrong through your parenting will only cause you to focus more energy on getting your child to act the way you want. While no one wants to reexperience the pain they endured as a child, correcting your negative core beliefs requires that you address your trauma. The more you learn how to meet your own needs, the more you'll be able to process your challenges in a way that builds your confidence in yourself, as a person first and as a parent second. Only by creating a healthy, loving relationship with yourself can you create a healthy, loving relationship with your child.

Practice Equals Positive Change

Just like the clients whose stories I've shared in this chapter, you are likely seeing parallels between how you parent and the way you were parented. Parenting through the past is a generational pattern, and you are caught in the middle—previously on the receiving end, you're now on the giving end. If you continue to parent from the past, your child may someday be in the exact same position that you're in today.

However, by recognizing the pattern and changing how you parent, you will be able to impact not only your child, but their potential children as well. In place of unmet needs, avoiding challenges, and emotional and behavioral outbursts, you have the opportunity to leave a legacy of hope, healing, and wholeness for generations to come. When you are willing to invest time and energy into addressing your trauma and the patterns it left behind, you'll not only learn how to parent more effectively but also bring positive change into all your relationships. Just as unmet needs create undesirable behavior, you'll find that once you learn to meet your own needs and parent in the present, the entire family benefits.

Part 3

How to Start Healing from the Past

Chapter 4

Learning to Self-Soothe

In chapter 3, we touched on the way that children learn to self-soothe (or self-regulate) through co-regulation with their parents. In recent years, self-soothing has become a major topic of interest, with parenting experts offering a wealth of tips and techniques for teaching babies to self-soothe.

The parent's ability to self-soothe is the most important factor in helping their child learn this skill. Unfortunately, very few parents have mastered this for themselves. The vast majority of parents I see can't slow down their racing thoughts or curb their emotional and impulsive behaviors without using unhealthy coping mechanisms. This may involve trying to gain control over the situation or their child, but if that doesn't work, a typical alternative is numbing via television, food, social media, or substances; in some cases, they may even resort to harming others or themselves.

As you've learned by now, the way you react toward your child has very little to do with them, and more to do with your previous pain and the negative core beliefs it gave you. Your ability to handle challenging situations is directly related to your ability to regulate your emotions when those challenging situations arise.

For adults, learning to self-soothe is a cyclical process. It starts with identifying what thoughts, events, or memories trigger intense emotions and overwhelm. But since digging into past traumas and negative experiences can be hard, it's important to have self-soothing tools in place before you begin so that you can regulate the emotions that come up. In short, you're learning and practicing self-soothing at the same time. Even if you think you can self-soothe, don't skip over this chapter—we all get better with practice. In fact, the tools are so important that I recommend reading this chapter more than once and working through the activities multiple times before you continue with the book.

The Window of Tolerance

The *window of tolerance* is a term coined by Dan Siegel (1999) that refers to a state of being in which you are able to function and thrive regardless of what is occurring around you. When you are in your window, you can calmly respond to situations, think logically, and intentionally choose how to respond. However, certain triggers can send you out of your window and into a state of either hyperarousal or hypoarousal.

The Window of Tolerance

Hyperarousal Zone	Defensiveness Racing thoughts Feeling unsafe Anger Impulsivity
Optimal Zone (The Window of Tolerance)	Able to feel and think simultaneously Feelings are tolerable Feeling safe Feeling open and curious Awareness of boundaries
Hypoarousal Zone	Feeling numb Crying Shutting down Flat affect Feeling ashamed

In a state of hyperarousal, you may experience racing thoughts, anger, agitation, yelling, anxiety, impulsivity, and overwhelm (Siegel, 1999). This condition occurs when the brain's fight-or-flight response is triggered by an internal event (such as feeling unheard or unsafe) or an external event (like witnessing violence or being physically controlled). Being hyperaroused can cause difficulties with sleeping, eating, and managing thoughts and emotions. At an extreme level, individuals may even dissociate by blacking out and losing control of themselves, leading to destructive behavior like fighting, road rage, or property damage.

On the opposite end of the spectrum is hypoarousal, which is characterized by self-isolating, crying, falling asleep, feeling ashamed or numb, or lacking energy. Being hypoaroused makes it hard to think clearly or remember events; it can send you into an "autopilot" mode or create the sensation of being separate from your body. On an extreme level, people may dissociate and appear checked out of a situation. This hypoaroused state reflects the brain's freeze response, which can be triggered when you sense external danger or feel internally threatened (Siegel, 1999). The brain activates the freeze response when it decides, within a matter of milliseconds, that doing nothing in the situation would be safer than fighting or fleeing. This can occur when the source of the threat seems too overwhelming or too powerful to fight or escape from. For instance, many clients who endured sexual assault as a child report "numbing" or "freezing" during the assault because they felt more harm would come from trying to escape or fight their abuser off.

Each person's window of tolerance is unique. Some people have narrow windows due to previous unresolved traumas, while others have wider windows and are better able to handle intense events and emotions.

Past events, especially childhood experiences, often dictate what causes someone to leave their window of tolerance and enter a state of hyperarousal or hypoarousal. One client told me that when she feels like she is not good enough, she will isolate from her friends and family for days, watch movies, eat junk food, and emotionally numb out (hypoarousal). Another client shared that when she fears someone might abandon her, she will lash out in anger, call them names, and emotionally push them away, all the while hoping they come back. Once she even dissociated and hit someone (hyperarousal). Being able to self-soothe requires getting familiar with your specific triggers and understanding which arousal zone they push you into.

Activity 4.1
Identifying Your Window

This activity will help you identify your specific triggers (i.e., the thoughts, feelings, and events that cause you to lose control), as well as the circumstances that help you stay in your window of tolerance. If you need help identifying your triggers, look back to activities 1.1 and 1.2—often unmet needs and core beliefs serve as triggers that kick you outside your window.

What puts you here:

Hyperarousal Zone

What helps you stay here:

**Optimal Zone
(The Window of
Tolerance)**

What puts you here:

Hypoarousal Zone

Widening and Returning to Your Window

Now that you've identified what keeps you in and pushes you out of your window of tolerance, it's time to learn how you can widen your window by increasing your ability to handle challenging situations, as well as ways to get back into your window (i.e., self-soothe) when you get in a state of hyper- or hypoarousal.

We all know someone who has what we politely call a "short fuse"—someone you're hesitant to share information with because they so often overreact. These are indicators of a small window of tolerance. The good news is that no matter what size your own window is, you can always expand it by developing your ability to handle challenging situations, stay emotionally regulated, and make thoughtful decisions. The following techniques will help you widen your window of tolerance.

Activity 4.2
Widening Your Window

The Arousal/Calm Method

This is a classic technique for widening your window. Simply follow these steps:

1. First, think about a mildly distressing thought. On a scale of 0 (no distress) to 10 (extreme distress), try to get your stress to a level 3.

2. Now close your eyes, release the thought, and focus on your breath. Place your hands on your belly and feel it slowly rise and fall. If another distressing thought comes up, direct your mind back to your breath and the rise and fall of your belly.

3. Do this activity until you are at a 0 on the distress scale, and repeat it several times a day.

4. Once you are able to emotionally regulate yourself after a level 3 situation, try it with a level 4 or 5 situation. Slowly move up the scale until you are at a level 9 and can still engage in a logical thought process and not become overwhelmed with emotions or racing thoughts.

   If your window of tolerance is on the narrow end, this activity will take weeks, if not months, of practice until you notice a difference. Give yourself time and grace—remember, you are literally rewiring your brain!

Ten-Minute Time-Out

Of course, you can't always pause your child's challenging behaviors until your window of tolerance is wider. With that in mind, another technique I recommend is taking a ten-minute time-out before responding to your child or making a parenting decision, especially if you're dealing with an undesirable behavior. In the heat of the moment, your brain instinctively looks for ways to meet your own needs. To refocus on what your child needs from you in that moment, remove yourself from the situation, take some deep breaths, and focus your thoughts on logical observations rather than your emotional interpretation. For example, you can tell yourself, *My child is really upset right now* as opposed to *My child doesn't respect me.*

Neutral, factual observations help your mind slow down, taming your emotions and the impulses they bring up, and provide you a larger context to work from. This is going to take a lot of practice, and you may find that you need more than ten minutes for it to work. Remember, widening your window of tolerance is not a one-and-done solution. Rather, it is a lifelong process that requires ongoing patience and persistence.

Even when you're working to widen your window of tolerance, there will be times when things get too overwhelming, pushing you out of your window. When that happens, the following self-soothing techniques will help you quickly return to your window. Of course, the goal is to eventually widen your window so this happens less and less often, but these simple and effective techniques will help get you through in the interim.

Activity 4.3
Returning to Your Window

Diaphragmatic Breathing

When you've left your window of tolerance, a great first step is to take several minutes to engage in diaphragmatic breathing, also known as belly breathing. Most people breathe from their chest, which means they take shorter, faster breaths that increase their blood pressure and heart rate. Diaphragmatic breathing, on the other hand, slows your heart rate, decreases your blood pressure, and increases the flow of oxygen to your brain. The more you can train yourself to breathe from your belly, the easier it will become to calm your racing thoughts.

To familiarize yourself with how diaphragmatic breathing feels, take a moment to go through the following steps:

1. Lie flat on your back and prop your knees up.

2. Place one hand on your chest and the other on your stomach. Take deep breaths in through your nose and out through your mouth, feeling your belly rise and fall.

3. Once you feel comfortable with the rhythm of your breath, count how long it takes to fill your stomach with air as you inhale. (It takes most people between three to five seconds.)

4. Now take that number and multiply it by two—this is the number you should count to when exhaling through your mouth. (For example, it takes me four seconds to inhale and eight seconds to exhale.) You'll notice that you have to drastically slow down your breath as your exhale—this is what helps your heart rate slow down. Additionally, while you are counting, your brain cannot think about the event that just happened or how you feel about it. Instead, all your energy is directed to your body.

Calm/Safe Place

Once you settle your body by deep breathing, you can further redirect your brain and create a sense of calm by practicing what is known as the calm/safe place, which is commonly used in a form of trauma treatment known as eye movement desensitization and reprocessing (EMDR; Shapiro, 2018). Here's how it works:

1. To start, close your eyes and imagine a place, real or imaginary, where you feel calm and safe.

2. While you are focusing on this place, engage as many senses as you can. Ask yourself, *What can I hear, see, taste, feel, and smell?*

3. I also recommend visualizing your body's physical location in your calm place. Perhaps you are sitting on a chair, standing on the beach, or lying in a hammock.

4. Stay in your place for several minutes until you feel you are back in your window of tolerance. You may need to practice this activity several times for it to be optimally effective, but each time you do it, it gets easier for your brain to believe you are really there.

Thoughtful Reflection

Once you've successfully returned to your window, it's time to identify what pushed you out of it. Reflect on these prompts:

1. What event happened right before you left your window of tolerance? For example, did your child slam their bedroom door or receive a bad grade on a test?

_____

_____

_____

_____

2. What emotions did you feel during that event and why? The most obvious answer is probably anger, but look for other emotions that might hide behind your anger. For example, were you fearful you were being disrespected? Embarrassed about your child's behavior? If you struggle to identify your emotions, see the appendix for a list of possible emotions that you can work from.

_____

_____

_____

_____

3. After identifying your emotions, explore whether the event reinforced a previous negative core belief, such as *I'm not good enough* or *I'm not wanted*. Remember, the events that cause us to leave our windows are usually triggers from negative childhood experiences.

_____

_____

_____

_____

4. Once you've identified your emotions and core beliefs, just sit still for a minute and calmly acknowledge them. Although people often attempt to avoid or numb themselves from uncomfortable thoughts and emotions, when you force yourself to think about the discomfort without judgment, it will prevent you from running from your emotions, thoughts, and feelings.

5. After you've returned to your window, think about what you, as a parent, need right now. Do you need to hear that you are doing a good job? Do you need reassurance that your child pushing you away doesn't mean you aren't wanted? Identifying and meeting your own needs in this moment is crucial to prevent you from misplacing them onto your child.

"How Does That Make You Feel?"

When teaching parents about their window of tolerance, I spend a lot of time talking about what emotions cause them to be angry. This may sound strange because anger is technically its own emotion, but I have never worked with a parent who is only angry at a situation with their child. Rather, they're experiencing many different emotions, and anger just happens to be the one they show. That's because society has taught us that it's okay to feel and express anger rather than diving deeper into more vulnerable feelings. The anger that people experience is usually not directed at the situation, but at a more vulnerable emotion the situation brings up for them, such as fear, guilt, shame, or embarrassment.

For example, imagine that you receive a phone call from your child's school, telling you that your child has been bullying someone. If someone asked you how you were feeling after that call, you might say that you're angry at your child for hurting others. However, underneath the anger, you could be feeling:

- Embarrassment that the child you raised would hurt someone else

- Shame that you are a "bad parent"

- Guilt that you may have missed connecting with your child

- Fear that your child is turning into a horrible person

Widening your window of tolerance requires acknowledging the deeper emotions that cause you to feel angry. An easy way to build this emotional intelligence is by reviewing the list of emotions in the appendix several times a day, particularly when you feel angry. For each emotion on the list, try to identify what types of situations or thoughts bring this emotion up for you. Each time you complete this activity, you are slowing your brain down rather than going straight to your fight-flight-freeze response, making it easier to return to your window of tolerance when you are distressed.

Parenting in Peace

Return for a moment to the imaginary phone call from your child's school about their behavior. Imagine that this time, instead of blowing up in anger, you step away from the situation, breathe from your belly, and identify the deeper emotions that are driving your anger. Instead of spiraling into anxiety over the future consequences of your child's behavior or how it reflects on your parenting, you calmly consider what your child could be going through and thoughtfully choose some different strategies to connect with them. Imagine lying in bed at night and, instead of wondering if you are making the same mistakes as your parent, feeling the peace of knowing that you did the best you could to meet your child's needs rather than your own.

Right now, you might not think this hypothetical situation is possible. But I'm thrilled to tell you that when you start healing from your past, changes like this are not just possible—they're inevitable. As Dan Siegel and Mary Hartzell write in *Parenting from the Inside Out* (2003), "Self-reflection and an understanding of our internal processes allows us to choose a greater range of responses to our children's behavior" (p. 68). The more you learn about your emotional patterns and practice bringing them under conscious control, the more natural it will feel to be present with your child and parent them without your past intervening.

Chapter 5

Sitting with the Past and Meeting Your Own Needs

Have you ever tried to forget an uncomfortable memory or numb the feelings that linger from a traumatic event? Many of us, myself included, have memories of our childhood that we would love to erase. The irony is that the more we attempt to avoid or dismiss the pain we experienced in the past, the more we suffer in the present. In order to heal your past wounds and be fully present when making parenting decisions, it is necessary to "sit with" your past: to reflect on the painful experience from your childhood and remember all the details involved.

When I tell a client they are going to sit with their past, it's normal for their eyes to widen and their mouth to frown—everything on their face screams, *I don't want to go back there!* While it can be incredibly difficult to reexperience past events, recalling these memories will help you process your triggers, giving you more space and energy to connect with your child.

To practice sitting with your past, you simply analyze a distressing memory from a nonjudgmental space, feel the emotions that come from the memory while staying in your window of tolerance, and consider how the event may still be impacting you. Instead of letting yourself get caught up in uncontrollable emotions (e.g., anger, sadness, fear) or illogical thoughts (e.g., "My mother was the worst person on the planet" or "My parents intentionally made my life hell"), you assume the role of a neutral observer. While it seems simple, it takes a lot of patience and practice. Like most of the skills in this book, sitting with the past is not a one-and-done event; it involves cultivating the continued ability to feel and think about the past in a logical way. But it's worth it—once this practice becomes routine, you'll be far less vulnerable to being triggered by the past.

For example, I once went through this exercise with a client who was struggling with feelings of inadequacy. When I asked her to identify a painful memory from her childhood, she described being three years old and sitting on the front porch when her mother came out to tell her that her father wasn't coming to pick her up. During the initial exercise, she cried uncontrollably and stated that she hated her father and that she was clearly not loved by anyone. Did it *feel* that way to her? Absolutely. Was it logical or accurate that no one loved her? No. After several therapy sessions of practicing sitting in the past, she was able to calmly describe the event to me and noted that while she felt sad about it, it wasn't her fault that her father didn't show up, nor could she have done anything to make him be a better dad.

The next series of activities will help you learn how to sit with your past, but before you begin, it's important to learn what sitting in the past is *not*:

- **Sitting with the past is not a way to blame your parents or others.** Placing blame amounts to you giving up your power to heal. Could others have done things differently? Sure! But dwelling on their issues won't make you feel better, and it won't heal your past.

- **Sitting with the past is not an opportunity for self-loathing, self-pity, or getting others to feel sorry for you.** Wallowing in your own misery just indulges the negative core beliefs that increase your tendency to parent through the past. If you're willing to learn, you can still heal from the past and live a fuller, happier life.

- **Sitting with the past is not intended to dismiss your experiences or feelings, or to condone what happened to you as a child.** Instead, it's meant to help you see how much of what you went through wasn't a reflection of you. Trying to understand a situation doesn't mean overlooking or condoning someone's behavior. It's simply letting your adult brain resolve the "lessons" your child brain took from the experience so that you can heal from it.

Five Steps to Sitting with the Past

The following pages provide a five-step series of activities that I've developed to help you sit with your past while remaining in your window of tolerance. Remember that this is not a one-and-done exercise—you will need to repeat it in its entirety several times, and I recommend using a separate journal to work through it. Take each step slowly and thoughtfully, giving your brain time to carefully think about the event without getting hijacked or shut down by your emotions. You can't change how you were parented or the unfair trials you went through, but you can reflect on your experiences and process how they made you feel as a child so you can decrease your emotional reactivity in the present. This is hard work, so please know that it doesn't make you beyond repair if you struggle with these activities. It will get easier with time.

Activity 5.1
Documenting the Past

Starting with the earliest memory you can remember, journal through every uncomfortable or traumatic event you recall from your childhood up to around 25 years of age. Write down as many *observable* details as you can about each event, including your age, the time and place, the actions of other people, and your actions. Leave out any description of emotions, thoughts, or assumptions. The goal here is to be a neutral observer of the events.

To help you get started, here's an example from my client Asher:

When I was three years old [age], *I was sitting on the front porch at my mom's house* [place]. *My father was supposed to pick up me and my big brother to go to lunch and buy us birthday presents. We waited for what felt like hours, but our father never came* [actions]. *We just sat until my mom and stepdad came out to cheer us up. I remember my brother cried, which made me cry, but I don't remember how the rest of the day went.*

Activity 5.2
Sitting with One Event

Now that you have documented as many uncomfortable events as you can from your past, I want you to select the *least* distressing memory to focus on. If you choose an event that is extremely distressing or hard for you to think about, you will leave your window of tolerance and shut down. Once you have selected the least distressing event, grab your journal and slowly answer the following questions. If you rush through your answers, you will not be able to help your brain slow down and allow the left and right hemispheres to communicate with each other. Read one question at a time, think about the answer for no less than two minutes, and then start writing.

After answering each question, I recommend you take some time to literally sit. Be still for a while with what you've just written. Your experiences have likely been dismissed by others in the past—you may have even dismissed them yourself. This time, let your answers be what they are. Don't try to change them, and don't let your negative core beliefs hijack your experience or illogical thoughts take over. This is how you learn to let your emotions have a voice.

1. While the event was occurring, what did you think about the event? (It's okay if you didn't think anything or don't remember what you thought.)

   Example: *I thought that something was wrong, but I don't think I knew what was wrong. I remember being confused, probably because I was three.*

   _____

   _____

   _____

   _____

   _____

2. What emotions do you remember experiencing during the event?

   Example: *I remember crying because I was sad. I remember getting ready for him to pick us up, and I was sad I didn't get to go.*

   _____

   _____

   _____

   _____

   _____

   _____

3. What do you currently think about the event? (It's normal and okay to have several different thoughts. Describe as many of them as you can, even if they conflict.)

   Example: *I think that my dad is a piece-of-crap excuse for a man. Who leaves two kids sitting on a front porch? But I also have come to realize that he didn't know how to be a dad. He probably had no clue that it hurt me so badly. But I still think that if he wanted to be around us, he would have shown up.*

   _____

   _____

   _____

   _____

   _____

   _____

4. What emotions do you currently have about the event? (It's okay to have numerous emotions, even some that conflict with each other.)

   Example: *I feel unwanted and rejected. I was a kid who just wanted to be like his dad, and he blew me off. I'm sad, embarrassed, and fearful that if my own dad didn't want to be with me, why would anyone else?*

5. What needs weren't met during the event? Remember that unmet needs can include psychological, emotional, and physical safety, comfort, and belonging. (Refer to activity 1.2 for your list of unmet needs. You may see some similarities between that list and this answer.)

   Example: *I didn't feel cared for, important, or wanted. I didn't feel loved or like I belonged to anyone.*

6. What challenges or uncomfortable emotions did you experience during the event?

Example: *I experienced a lot of disappointment because he never showed up. I would get my hopes up and then be disappointed. My first memory was being rejected.*

_____

_____

_____

_____

_____

Activity 5.3
Identifying the Support You Needed

Typically, you have unmet needs from your past because you either (1) didn't know how to verbally ask for what you needed or (2) asked for your needs to be met, but your parents dismissed you or didn't know how to meet them. In this activity, you'll identify what support you needed at the time of the event that you didn't receive. This may be challenging and emotional for you, so take as many breaks as you need and continue to work on staying in your window of tolerance.

1. Based on your answers in activity 5.2, write what you would have liked an adult (not any adult involved in the memory) to say or do for you during that event. What did you need to hear from someone?

   Example: *I really needed to be told it wasn't my fault, that I wasn't the reason my father didn't show up. I needed someone to sit with me and tell me I could be sad or upset, but also tell me that he didn't know how to do what he promised. I guess I mostly wanted to be held and told I was a great kid who was important and wanted.*

2. Now ask yourself, *Do I still have these needs today?* Bear in mind that you may intellectually know that those needs are met, but still not *feel* that they are. Another way to ask the question is, *Would I emotionally benefit from someone saying these things to me today?* (Chances are, you would.)

   Example: *Yeah. I still want to be told that I'm wanted and that I'm a good person. I think knowing these things would take a huge weight off my shoulders.*

Activity 5.4
Providing Yourself with What You Need

Now that you've identified what support you needed in the past, it's important to start meeting those needs now so you don't push them onto your children. In this activity, you will write a letter to the "you" who experienced your distressing memory. You will tell that past version of you exactly what you needed to hear from a trusted, loving adult after the event occurred. Here is an excerpt from the letter Asher wrote to his younger self:

Dear three-year-old Asher,

I'm so sorry your dad didn't show up when he said he would. You didn't deserve disappointment that young, and I understand if you're sad or angry. I'd love to spend time with you because you are a really cool kid. Life is going to work out for you. It'll be hard, but it'll be worth it. Don't let him make you bitter or guarded. Love the family that is here for you, because they are doing everything they can for you.

This is only a brief example of what a letter to yourself might look like. It's okay if yours is more detailed or rambles on—focus on saying what is in your heart and what you need to hear.

_____

_____

_____

_____

_____

_____

_____

_____

_____

_____

_____

Once your letter is written, look back at the unmet needs you described in activity 5.3 and think of a few ways you can fulfill those needs for yourself. Here's an example from Asher's list:

Unmet Need	Ways to Meet This Need
I needed to be told it wasn't my fault and to have someone sit with me.	*Read my letter out loud so I can really hear what I needed to be told in that moment.* *Take myself out for that lunch my father promised.*

If there are specific experiences that you cannot recreate, such as *I needed someone to show up to my third-grade dance recital*, focus on the feelings you would have had in that memory—what else could you do that will make you feel the way you felt as a child in dance class, while treating yourself the way a proud parent would have? This may sound a little "out there," but I promise it works! Try it for yourself:

Unmet Need	Ways to Meet This Need

Activity 5.5
Why Did These Things Happen?

The previous steps were more focused on identifying your emotions, while this step is about using the logical side of your brain. To do so, return to the traumatic memory you described and consider why it might have happened—what could have caused or contributed to the event? Try not to rush through with reductive statements like "because my parents were horrible" or "because nobody wanted me." Really explore all the possible factors. The more you engage the logical side of your brain, the less reactivity you will experience in the present.

1. Why do you think this event happened? Try to answer from a calm, neutral, logical perspective.

   Example: *I actually talked to my father about ten years ago, because I needed to understand why he hated me and didn't love me. He stated that he never had a dad, and his mother's boyfriends were very abusive. He didn't know what to do as a parent, so he left. Logically, I believe him—he abandoned me because he experienced that in his childhood.*

2. After considering these possibilities, what thoughts and emotions do you have about the event? Compare what you're thinking and feeling now to your answers to questions 3 and 4 in activity 5.2. Have any of your thoughts and emotions about the event changed? (It's okay if they have or if they haven't.)

Example: *My answers have changed slightly. I still think he was a crappy dad and could have figured out how to be better, but I think I understand why he did what he did. To me, understanding his reasons is different from accepting his behavior. I still think that if he wanted to be around us, he would have shown up. But I don't feel as unwanted and rejected as I did before. If I weren't his kid, he would have done the same thing to someone else. His actions say more about him than they do me.*

My goal with this exercise isn't to dismiss your feelings, experiences, or trauma. It's also not intended to excuse, overlook, or condone what happened to you as a child. Instead, it's meant to help you see that what you went through is no reflection on you. If someone told you that what happened was your fault, I'm here to tell you it wasn't. Your ability to understand a situation doesn't overlook or dismiss someone's behavior; it helps you move on from it.

When you're done, I want you to repeat activities 5.2 through 5.5 with every event you wrote about in activity 5.1. Each time you repeat the exercise, choose an event that is more distressing than the one you just sat with. Working incrementally through distressing events will help you remain in your window of tolerance.

Meeting Your Own Needs

Along with helping you process painful memories, sitting with the past helps you learn what your childhood can teach you about your current needs and how you can fulfill them yourself. You already began this work in the previous activity, and the following tools will help you to fulfill your needs at an even deeper level—to give yourself love in ways that resonate with who you are today.

The Five Love Languages

Each of us has an innate preference for how love is shown to us. Gary Chapman's book *The Five Love Languages* (2015) outlines five primary modalities, or languages, through which people give and receive love: physical touch, quality time, acts of service, receiving gifts, and words of affirmation. If you aren't aware of your love language, you can take the online quiz at https://5lovelanguages.com. Knowing your personal love language (or languages) is incredibly useful for understanding the root of your needs and finding ways to meet them. The following list offers some ideas for how to meet your needs in ways that truly speak to you, but the options are unlimited.

- **Physical touch:** Book a massage; take a bubble bath; moisturize your skin.

- **Quality time:** Spend time alone doing something you enjoy, such as doing a puzzle, taking an evening stroll, working out at the gym, or taking yourself to a movie.

- **Acts of service:** Hire someone to help you complete weekly or monthly responsibilities (such as a housekeeper or landscaper); get your nails or hair done; clean or redecorate to create a nurturing home environment.

- **Receiving gifts:** Buy yourself flowers; invest in a learning opportunity by enrolling in an online course or workshop that interests you; splurge on an item you've wanted for a while.

- **Words of affirmation:** Write caring notes to yourself; create a daily gratitude list; repeat affirmations out loud to yourself; engage in positive self-talk.

Try showing love to yourself through your love language on a weekly basis—you will be surprised at what a difference it makes. Parents who show forms of love toward themselves report feeling happier and more fulfilled (Chapman, 2014). Additionally, I have seen that children who witness their parents saying and doing kind things for themselves will engage in similar habits.

Four Areas of Self-Care

The concept of self-care is often misunderstood as a way to pamper yourself that is selfish and self-indulgent. This is, in part, because Western culture has turned being overworked and exhausted into a status symbol and framed people who engage in self-care as lazy, selfish, or not committed enough. However, as you may have experienced, not engaging in self-care is a recipe for becoming easily irritated, upset, and burned out. That's why I look at self-care as a necessary means of protecting and enhancing your mental and physical health.

Still, it's important to learn what activities truly leave you feeling restored and replenished, as opposed to guilty or overindulgent. It's also important to recognize that not everyone will engage in self-care the same way. For example, cleaning and organizing might be one person's self-care, while going for a run or a bicycle ride is more effective for another person.

The following list describes four areas of self-care you should tend to on a regular basis, along with ideas for specific activities you can use. Some are more challenging than others—as always, practice and consistency are the key to seeing (and feeling) results.

- **Emotional self-care** involves maintaining your heart and soul. When I ask my clients what they feel through the majority of the day, many don't know how to answer; their busy schedules and many demands lead them to suppress their emotions to just get through the day. Ruminating on uncomfortable emotions isn't any better than suppressing them. Instead, take several three-minute breaks throughout each day to think about how you are feeling and why you feel this way. Identifying your emotions and what triggered them can help you learn about yourself and pinpoint solutions to process discomfort.

- **Physical self-care** involves checking in with your body and giving it what it needs. When life becomes overwhelming and hectic, it's easy to default to fast food, lack of sleep, sitting too long in front of a computer, and other habits that contribute to general discomfort. If you notice a growing sense of tension or sluggishness, review your daily habits, including the food you consume, the amount of water you drink, the number of hours you sleep at night, and the type and frequency of exercise you perform (aim for at least 30 minutes each day doing any physical activity you enjoy).

- **Psychological self-care** is about monitoring your thoughts, especially the ones that come up a lot. As you've learned, what you think about influences your emotions and behaviors (and vice versa), making this one of the most beneficial forms of self-care. To start, select one thought you have about yourself or a situation you are in. Ask yourself, *Is this thought positive, helpful, and true?* If you can't say yes to all three, it's time to challenge the thought and find another to put in its place. For example, *I'm a terrible parent* is not true (even if you feel like it is), and it's certainly not positive or helpful. Consciously discard that thought and replace it with one that is accurate and nurturing, such as, *I'm doing the best I can* or *Today has been difficult, but it's helped me learn how to improve.*

- **Spiritual self-care** is the practice of engaging in a positive way with your faith, spirituality, or other way of making meaning. For some, attending church or other religious gatherings is fulfilling and helpful, while practices such as meditation, prayer, or mindfulness work better for others. Some nourish their spirit by spending time in nature, perhaps by going for a hike or sitting quietly by a river. If you don't know where to start, simply ask yourself, *What does my soul need today?* and do whatever comes to mind.

Getting What You Need to Give

Strange as it may seem right now, sitting with your past and meeting your own needs are foundational to creating the relationship you want with your child. By reflecting on your past, you have an opportunity to confront the lies your brain has been telling you about who you are and what you need. And by learning your love languages and filling your own cup with self-care activities, you're empowering and equipping yourself to pour into your child's life.

Chapter 6

Your Core Beliefs and Self-Esteem

In chapter 1, you identified the core beliefs you have about yourself based on your past experiences. These beliefs often take the form of "I am" statements, such as *I am worthless, I am powerless,* or *I am a horrible person*. Along with core beliefs that you hold about yourself, you also hold beliefs about other people, the world, and the future, which play a central role in the parenting choices you make. When these beliefs are clouded by negativity, it can decrease self-esteem, increase pessimism, and lower your confidence in your parenting skills, making you more likely to get angry at your children or simply feel like giving up. This chapter will help you recognize those negative beliefs, challenge them, and replace them with beliefs that increase your confidence as a person and as a parent.

"People Are . . ."

Beliefs like *People won't like me if they know me, My partner will leave me eventually,* or *My kids don't respect me* didn't start with the people currently in your life. In all likelihood, they first showed up in response to childhood pain. For example, being bullied in grade school could easily have led to a negative core belief of *No one likes me.* Like all core beliefs, your brain held on to this idea to give you an explanation for what happened to you and help you predict (and avoid) that pain in the future. Today, however, this belief will negatively impact your parenting by leading you to assume that your child doesn't like you.

For example, Latonya was raised with six older brothers and, unsurprisingly, grew up struggling to be heard in her family. This resulted in the core belief "No one listens to me." Now she was in the same position again, with an eight-year-old daughter who behaved defiantly and refused to follow directions. When I asked Latonya if she felt that this core belief about others was impacting how she responded to her daughter, she agreed completely. "I had to yell and scream to get any attention as a kid," she explained. "Now, when my daughter doesn't listen, the quickest and easiest method is to start yelling. I want someone to listen to me."

"The World Is . . ."

As children, the events we witness in our immediate environment, especially the things we see happen to other people, shape our perceptions of the world in general. For example, a child who sees the soccer coach yelling at and ridiculing the players may form the belief that all coaches are mean, while children who witness natural disasters or violence on the news may conclude that the world is a scary place. Common beliefs about the world include *I need control to be safe, The world is out to get people like me,* and *Life isn't fair.*

For example, Roy refused to let his fourteen-year-old son take a solo airplane trip to visit a family member in another state. Something bad could happen on the trip, Roy insisted, and if it did, his son was simply too young to manage alone. Even in our therapy session, Roy couldn't help pressing the point to his son: "The world is dangerous! How come you don't see that?"

Roy revealed later in our session that he had been a flight attendant at the time of the 9/11 attacks. In fact, he'd been on a flight to New York when they had an emergency landing. This experience left him convinced that the world isn't safe and that no one will help if something bad happens. These beliefs were now guiding his parenting choices.

"The Future Is . . ."

"Dr. Brie, how do you know something terrible won't happen to my child?"

I'm asked this question on an almost weekly basis. It's surprising how many parents struggle to feel optimistic about their child's future—many of them use words like *bleak*, *terrifying*, or *hopeless* when I ask them to describe their feelings about it. One parent even said, "You can't make me think about the future, Dr. Brie!" Just the idea caused them to shut down.

My answer to the question above is always the same: "I *don't* know that. I can't guarantee nothing terrible will happen to your child. But not allowing your child to experience life because you're fearful of what might happen is meeting your needs, not theirs." Making your child engage in specific activities or denying them opportunities may seem like a way to control their future for their own good, but it will only create a child who lashes out, begins to rebel, or hides things from you.

Identifying Your Beliefs

Very rarely are parents consciously aware of their core beliefs and how those beliefs are impacting their parenting. But identifying and acknowledging your core beliefs is incredibly important for several reasons. First, these core beliefs are no longer "hidden" somewhere in your brain. Rather, you are able to bring them to the forefront of your mind, which allows you to start replacing incorrect or negative beliefs. Second, when your core beliefs are not true or helpful, it can cause your self-worth and confidence to decrease over time. By identifying these beliefs, you can develop more constructive and positive thoughts that decrease your chances of engaging in unhelpful parenting choices and allow you to connect with your child in more meaningful ways.

Activity 6.1
Identifying Outward-Facing Core Beliefs

The following exercise will help you start identifying the outward-facing core beliefs that are impacting your parenting. Depending on your age and life experience, this activity may take you hours or even days to complete. Along with taking your time, I suggest you monitor your uncomfortable emotions over the following week. If you feel angry, sad, uncomfortable, or upset, take a time-out to work through this activity with the event that triggered those feelings. It is likely that your brain is using its interpretation of the event to strengthen one of your negative core beliefs.

"People Are . . ."

Identify a past event that causes an uncomfortable emotion.

Example: *My dad broke promises to me as a kid.*

What does this say about other people?

Example: *Others won't be there for me or to help me.*

What core belief does this reflect?

Example: *Other people are liars and untrustworthy.*

"The World Is . . ."

Identify a past or current event that causes an uncomfortable emotion.

Example: *My child got bullied at school.*

What does this say about the world?

Example: *The world is full of awful people. The world is out to get us.*

What core belief does this reflect?

Example: *The world is dangerous and unpredictable.*

_____

_____

_____

"The Future Is . . ."

Identify a current event that causes an uncomfortable emotion.

Example: *My boss skipped over me for a promotion.*

_____

_____

_____

What does this event say about your future?

Example: *I'm never going to excel, regardless of how hard I work. The future isn't within my control.*

_____

_____

_____

_____

What core belief does this reflect?

Example: *The future is hopeless and not worth fighting for.*

_____

_____

_____

_____

_____

Intergenerational Patterns of Core Beliefs

I once heard a mom jokingly mumble, "People suck!" while stuck in traffic with her young son. The next day, that same mom told me, the little boy had said, "People suck!" while strapped in his booster seat in his dad's truck.

This example reflects the reality that core beliefs can also come from generational patterns of thinking. As we've discussed, children can be very receptive to their parents' thoughts and behaviors, and if you have negative core beliefs about yourself and your environment, your child is likely to develop similar core beliefs. Some beliefs don't even need to be said aloud for your child to perceive them. For instance, a parent who shows signs of concern while spending the weekend working on the family budget is portraying the following message: "We have no money." In turn, the child can develop and internalize a core belief related to financial scarcity. Similar core beliefs can emerge if a parent exhibits insecurities related to body weight, wrinkles, strength, intelligence, success, and more.

Think for a moment about an aspect of life that you frequently criticize or simply have negative feelings about. Perhaps it has to do with certain types of people or the way the world works. Is it similar to something your parent was critical of? Whatever it is, be aware that your dissatisfaction with this aspect of life could end up becoming one of your child's negative core beliefs.

Self-Esteem

Unsurprisingly, the family and environment you grew up in has a long-term impact on the opinion you have about yourself and your worth as a person (Orth, 2018). Studies show that factors like parental warmth, low maternal depression, and the presence of a father contribute to the development of high self-esteem (Krauss et al., 2020). On the other hand, if a family environment is full of hostility, anger, unpredictability, or extreme sadness, children are more likely to develop low self-esteem and the negative core beliefs that accompany it.

Think about some of the personal insecurities you have. Do you criticize yourself for gaining weight, or gripe when new wrinkles show up on your face? Do you feel like your lack of intelligence holds you back, or like success always eludes you? Consider whether you noticed any of those self-critiques from the adults you grew up around. (And remember, they don't have to be said out loud for a child to perceive them.) The logic is simple—when a parent speaks negatively about themselves or their place in the world, a child will reason, *If my parent doesn't think positive things about themselves, I must be just as bad off as they are, if not worse*. This impact doesn't end with childhood—low self-esteem follows a person into adulthood and, among other things, influences how they raise their own children.

Along with impacting your child's self-perception, both now and in the future, low self-esteem has several negative consequences for your parenting success. One obvious consequence is that it makes you more likely to doubt your ability to successfully parent your child (Gondoli & Silverberg, 1997; Umaña-Taylor et al., 2013). It can also lead you to build your self-esteem through your child's achievements (Wuyts et al., 2015), bringing a double impact for the parent-child relationship. Not only does this create extra pressure for your child to make you proud, but it also sets both of you up for a drop in self-esteem anytime your child falls short of success.

Strength Through Self-Worth

Considering how much your self-esteem influences the way you parent, it's no surprise that parents who routinely parent through the past also report low self-esteem. Even those committed to learning how to parent in the present can get overly focused on what their efforts say about their worthiness; the mistakes and failures that naturally occur during the learning process can trigger negative core beliefs that lead parents right back to old habits of parenting through the past. The next chapter will show how you can increase your self-esteem to improve your parenting, model high self-worth for your child, and strengthen your relationship with them.

Chapter 7

Replacing Core Beliefs and Increasing Your Self-Esteem

"How do you think your core belief of *I'm not good enough* influences your parenting?" I asked my client Alexia.

"I just want everyone to be happy," she answered. "I say yes to all the things because I don't want anyone to be upset."

"So, if your kids are upset because you said no, what would it mean?"

"That I'm not doing a good job."

There are two ways parents can try to prove their negative core beliefs wrong or, at least, ensure they never "come true." The first way is to try to alter undesirable behaviors from their child that trigger the negative belief. The thought process goes something like, *If only my kid would* [insert desirable behavior], *then I won't* [insert negative core belief]. However, this approach is doomed to fail because you can't control other people's behaviors.

The second way—the only way that works—is to change your negative core belief by challenging it yourself and intentionally replacing the negative belief with one that is positive, helpful, and true. To begin this process, it's important to realize when your negative core belief pops up and to take steps to immediately address it, right then and there. This takes considerable practice before it becomes an automatic practice, so I recommend that you get into the habit by setting an alarm to check in with yourself three times during the day—midmorning (about 10 a.m.), before dinner (about 5 p.m.), and after your child goes to bed (around 9 p.m.). Each time the alarm goes off, ask yourself, *Have I felt like* [insert negative core belief] *recently?* If the answer is yes, write down the reason you felt this was true. Next, you will replace this belief with a statement that is more beneficial and accurate.

Here is an example to further clarify how this works. Joan, the mother of ten-year-old Stella, was seeking help with handling her daughter's chronic stomachaches and meltdowns during her morning drop-off at school. Interestingly, these behaviors only happened around Joan; Stella didn't push back or complain of stomach pain when her father was present.

During one session, Joan described her own childhood as awful. She reported that she rarely received any affection or comfort when she was upset or sad and was typically told "no" when she wanted a special treat or reward. Wanting to parent the opposite of how she was raised, Joan's efforts to be a good mom translated as an inability to set boundaries with her daughter. In turn, not only did Stella learn that her mother would placate her if she pushed back, but she also knew that Joan would rush to "help" her with any and all projects or tasks.

After learning about Joan's past and identifying how she was parenting through it, I asked Joan to set an alarm for specific times of the day. During these check-ins, Joan would sit alone for five to ten minutes and reflect on her negative core beliefs—*I'm not good enough* and *I'm supposed to make people happy*. Within a week, Joan reported that she was feeling these two core beliefs at least ten times a day, which naturally influenced her pattern of overly accommodating Stella whenever she complained or pushed back.

Throughout the next week, I had Joan practice replacing her negative core beliefs during these check-ins. In one situation, Joan reported thinking that she needed to clean Stella's room for her in order to make her daughter happy. Rather than thinking, *I need to make Stella happy*, she came up with a more accurate and helpful replacement belief: *I'm a mother; I don't need to do everything for my kids.* Joan was beginning to realize that Stella needed to learn how to meet her own needs and that the only way Joan could teach her was by having Stella do things herself.

Like Joan, you may be working tirelessly to counteract your negative core beliefs by parenting through your past. As you've probably discovered, the more you do this, the worse it gets. But by taking time to do check-ins, you can take back control over how you feel about yourself instead of letting others—including your child—dictate it for you. You can stop trying to earn acceptance and validation from others, leaving you free to focus on your child's needs rather than your own.

Now you might be thinking, *Dr. Brie, I don't have an extra 30 minutes a day to reflect on my thoughts and change them.* That's okay! Being a parent is incredibly demanding, so if you can't commit to three daily check-ins, see if committing to one is more feasible. Checking in with yourself even once a day can train your brain to readily identify your core beliefs when they come up. Start with what you can manage and slowly add more check-ins when you have time.

The remainder of this chapter will provide you with additional activities you can use to challenge and alter your negative beliefs.

Activity 7.1
Replacing Core Beliefs

Time to start replacing your negative core beliefs! To begin, choose one of the core beliefs you identified in chapter 1 (about yourself) or chapter 6 (about other people, the world, or the future) that you would like to change. Next, think of a neutral or positive belief you would rather have. For example, the core belief *No one wants me* can be changed to *I am wanted and loved*. Then, start reinforcing your new belief by noting three events that help confirm it. A word of caution: Avoid trying to come up with new core beliefs that are unrealistic, such as *I'm a perfect parent* or *I'm not making any mistakes*. Trying to believe your way to reaching unattainable standards will cause your brain to return to your initial core belief.

Core belief: _____

_____

_____

What was happening at the time that caused this belief to arise?

_____

_____

_____

What belief would you rather have?

_____

_____

_____

Describe three recent events that helped you feel that your new core belief is accurate (even just a little):

1. _____

_____

_____

_____

2. _____

_____

_____

_____

3. _____

_____

_____

_____

It's worth noting that writing down these three instances won't make you immediately believe your new core belief. However, it will allow your brain to start acknowledging that your negative core belief isn't 100 percent true. The more you can pause and acknowledge moments when your negative core belief was proven wrong, the more of these moments you will see, making your brain more open to the new belief you're bringing in.

Activity 7.2
Challenging Your Core Beliefs

Sometimes people have believed a negative core belief for so long that they can't even think of something they would rather believe. After all, there is nothing that the human brain loves more than predictability. In fact, the brain would rather say, *See, I knew it—I'm not good enough* than *Wow! I was wrong—I* am *good enough*. To get your brain more comfortable with letting go of your negative core beliefs, you have to show your brain that the new core belief can also be predictable.

To do so, select a core belief that you would like to challenge. Next, choose an action that will allow you to test out your belief, and write down what you think will happen as a result. After you take the action, write down what actually happened, and think about a new core belief suggested by the outcome. It's okay if you don't fully believe the new belief right away; the main goal is just to challenge the old one.

Here is an example:

Core belief tested: *I am not wanted.*

How to test your belief: *Reach out to five friends or family members and set up a virtual or in-person coffee date.*

Prediction: *Everyone will say they're busy or make some excuse to not spend time with me.*

What actually occurred: *Three friends and one family member planned a coffee date within a month, and one family member said she had too much on her plate.*

Thoughts about what occurred: *I'm not as unwanted as I thought; also, some people really do have a lot going on and can't prioritize time with their loved ones right now.*

New core belief: *I am wanted by some people and should invest in quality relationships. I am a good person, and some people enjoy being around me.*

Now it's your turn:

Core belief tested: _____

_____

_____

_____

How to test your belief: _____

_____

_____

_____

Prediction: _____

_____

_____

_____

What actually occurred: _____

_____

_____

_____

Thoughts about what occurred: _____

_____

_____

_____

_____

New core belief: _____

_____

_____

_____

_____

Over the coming weeks, repeat this activity with every core belief you would like to change. You can also test the same negative belief over and over with different actions. The more your old core belief is proved wrong, the more your brain will predict the new positive belief.

Activity 7.3
Time-In

Challenging and replacing core beliefs is much easier to do when you're in your window of tolerance. That's because when you're out of your window, the frontal lobe of your brain shuts off, making it much harder to brainstorm alternatives. For that reason, I recommend doing the previous two activities when you are calm, in your window, and able to logically think about your triggers and core beliefs.

However, there will likely be times when you are triggered in a situation with your child and need to alter your core beliefs right then and there. Every parent knows that not only can an argument with your child happen at any moment, but it can also be close to impossible to identify what caused the argument or how it spiraled so quickly. When this happens, it is crucial to take a step back from the situation so you can consider your reaction from a logical mindset, rather than an emotional one. I call this taking a "time-in." This activity is intended to slow down the argument and give you time to identify what is triggering you.

1. What emotions are you currently feeling?

    Example: *Sadness, anger, disrespect, and disappointment*

2. What occurred that is causing you to feel these emotions?

   Example: *I asked Tyler to clean up his mess in the kitchen. He said that other people leave a mess around the house and I don't bother them. I asked him not to worry about how I parent his siblings and do as I ask. He threw the dish into the sink and it broke. He stormed off and slammed his door.*

   _____

   _____

   _____

   _____

   _____

3. Why does this event bother or upset you? Explain your thoughts and reflections on the situation.

   Example: *Tyler seems really selfish. He doesn't help the household, and to top it off, he criticizes how I parent and takes a personal jab at me. I'm also hurt that he would break a dish and not apologize. He knows better! It seems like he thinks the world revolves around him, and the selfishness is getting awful.*

   _____

   _____

   _____

   _____

   _____

4. Reviewing your answer to question 3, what do you believe these statements say about you? What do they mean about you as a parent? Get specific here.

Example: *I believe Tyler's selfishness says that I'm a bad parent, that I failed him, and that he doesn't respect me. Maybe he's right that I don't parent my other kids the same. Maybe I do suck as a parent. I'm raising an entitled kid and that scares me. I don't want people thinking that I failed as a parent.*

5. What negative core belief was triggered in response to this event and why?

Example: *"I'm not a good enough parent" and "I failed as a parent" are the biggest ones. Logically, I know these likely aren't true, but they feel true because I think if I were raising Tyler the right way, he would listen to me.*

6. What are some other possible explanations for why the event happened? You can write down as many options as you want, regardless of how true or likely they seem.

   Example: *It's possible that Tyler had a bad day at school and took it out on me. Maybe he's feeling jealous of his siblings or feels like he is treated unfairly in the family. Maybe he thinks I love the other kids more.*

   _____

   _____

   _____

   _____

7. Considering these alternative explanations, what is a more realistic and helpful core belief that you can consider instead? Provide some facts to support the new belief. This new belief doesn't have to feel completely true; it's enough if it just feels possible.

   Example: *I am a good enough parent. I am doing the best job I can with three other kids in the house and a full-time job. I'm not doing everything "right," but that's okay. Each day is a chance to try again. One fight with my son doesn't mean I have failed. He is allowed to have a bad day and be upset. I'm not being rejected; I'm likely missing crucial information to help fix the situation. Tyler doesn't normally respond that way, so something else must be going on. It isn't all about me.*

   _____

   _____

   _____

   _____

Retrain Your Brain

As you've probably learned through experience, attempting to prove your negative core beliefs wrong by parenting through your past never creates lasting change. At best, your child's improved behavior changes your belief for just a couple hours, only to let you down later. At worst, your negative core belief is strengthened by your child's behavior. Replacing your negative beliefs may be very challenging at times, and you may need to reread a chapter or two or work through the activities often. But if you feel discouraged, remember that you are attempting to change beliefs that have been ingrained in your brain for decades! With persistence and dedication, you will change your negative core beliefs, tune into what your child is needing, and experience a relationship with your child that you never thought was possible.

Part 4

How to Parent
the Child
You Have

Chapter 8

Parenting Goals versus Parenting Intentions

If you could accomplish one thing with your parenting, what would it be? Raising a child who won't live with you in their thirties? Making sure your child doesn't hate you? Bringing up respectful kids who honor the family name?

Whether you've openly identified it or not, you likely have at least one goal you would like to achieve before your child leaves the nest. In fact, every parent I've ever worked with has a dream or goal for their child, regardless of whether they admit it.

Parenting goals can be classified into three different categories (Burns et al., 1984; Dix, 1992; Hastings & Grusec, 1998):

- **Parent-centered goals** are intended to give the parent the ability to control, change, or end their child's behavior in a way that meets the parent's agenda. These goals often sound like "I need to have a clean child," "I need silence," or "I need my child to listen."

- **Child-centered goals** are intended to instill certain values into the child, teach them lessons for their benefit, or increase their happiness. These goals may include "My child needs to learn the value of hard work," "I want to find out what's making my child angry," or "My child should apologize when they do something wrong."

- **Relationship-centered goals** are aimed at reaching a fair and equal solution during an interaction, wanting everyone to be happy in a situation, or building love, trust, and closeness. Examples include "I want us to have fun together" and "I would love for my child to know I'll always be there for them."

Some of these goals don't sound so bad, do they? However, in my practice I advocate for abandoning all goals and instead shifting to parenting *intentions*. There are several reasons for this.

First, even though each goal category has different intentions behind it, whenever a parent becomes focused on a specific goal or outcome for their child, they tend to project their own insecurities, fears, and doubts onto the child, creating an environment in which the child feels stifled, blamed, and criticized.

Second, the problem with setting goals that *you* would like your child to achieve is that it's not your child's job to make you happy or proud. It is important to remember that you gave life to (or adopted) a human being with their own unique personality, thoughts, ideas, goals, and aspirations.

Third, raising a child shouldn't feel like a to-do list. Instead, it should be about connection, growth, love, and compassion. Achieving goals may make you feel good for a while, but eventually, the feeling wears off. Parenting goals are no different. If your goal is to raise a "successful child," you'll likely be thrilled about their college acceptance letters for a day or two, but before long, you'll shift to thinking about the next big milestone that will make them successful.

Finally, the word *goal* suggests something that you can achieve if you just work hard enough. But the reality is that you cannot make your child do anything; in other words, you'll never be able to accomplish any goal you want for your child without their willing participation. And as we all know, your child may be a willing participant one day, only to become fiercely resistant the next. When this boundary-pushing occurs, many parents become upset, frustrated, or disappointed in their child and resort to discipline or guilt-tripping to nudge their child toward their own goal. However, it's important to remember that it's normal and developmentally appropriate for children to push boundaries as they attempt to discover who they want to be or what will make them happy. Creating unnecessary pressure for your child by setting goals for them will only slowly deteriorate the connection between you, sending a message that they cannot be fully loved unless they achieve your goals. Since every child wants their parent to be proud of them, there are only two possible outcomes: Either they consciously make choices just to make you happy, or they rebel against the pressure while hoping you learn to love the person they truly are.

Intentionally Parent the Child You Have

Understanding and letting your child be who they are—rather than parenting to get your goals met—is the essence of parenting the child you have. In contrast to setting goals that focus on *training* your child to behave the way you'd like, you create parenting intentions focused on *learning* about your child while *embodying* the personality traits that can help your child grow and develop. For example, rather than parenting with the goal of making your child calm down and be happy, parenting with the intention of calmness and curiosity will help you become inquisitive about your child's anger. This intention will also help you model for your child how to regulate their own emotions, as opposed to you telling them how to behave. This approach is much more conducive to learning, as it gives them an environment where they can discover their own talents and skills and grow in creative and productive ways.

At this point, you might be thinking, *Dr. Brie, you just spent seven chapters explaining to me how I need to focus more on my child rather than my past unmet needs, and now you're telling me to focus on* me?

It's true—I do want you to focus on your child's needs, but you can only do this when you create an environment in which your child can share their needs. Trying to parent the child you want into existence is never going to encourage the child you have to show you who they are. That kind of relationship can only come about through the way you interact with, interpret, and respond to your child.

As you've heard me say so many times by now, parenting the child you have is not a one-and-done fix for your child's problematic behavior. The methods I'm about to share should be thoughtfully used throughout each day. It will be challenging at first, like speaking a new language, but it will get easier as time goes on and you develop more confidence as you see improvements in yourself, your child, and your relationship. You will make mistakes and slide into old habits, but even that is great news— mistakes are proof that you are trying.

Identifying Parenting Intentions

Before you start choosing the intentions you want to bring to your parenting, it's important to understand the hidden factors that can make good intentions go bad:

- **Just like goals, your unmet needs from childhood can subtly dictate the intentions you choose.** For example, my client Kathy initially set this parenting intention: *I want to be kind* *and never yell at my kids.* When I asked how she came up with this intention, Kathy explained that she grew up watching her mother scream and yell at the smallest things Kathy did wrong. Although "never yelling" is certainly a good intention, Kathy had already slipped into parenting the child she was, not the children she had. After recognizing her unrealistic standard, Kathy developed a new intention: *I want to be slow to anger by recognizing the fears I have regarding my children.*

• **Your thoughts about your child will impact your parenting intentions.** When you're stuck on a thought like *My kid is selfish and I want to change that*, it can be hard to switch to a different thought, like *My child has unmet needs that I want to be more curious about.* For example, Edgar woke up every day with the goal of making his children happy, which not only caused him to answer yes to almost any request his children had, but also taught him to see his children as entitled and ungrateful. Instead of this unachievable goal, Edgar's new intention became *I want to provide balance in my children's lives by showing delayed gratification.*

• **Finally, the intentions you have for parenting should match the behaviors and characteristics you model for your child.** After working as a therapist for several years, I realized that I could learn how parents behaved in the home simply by observing and talking to their children. How? Because children model almost everything their parents say and do (including fun words you've heard them repeat when they shouldn't!).

Is Your Childhood Dictating Your Parenting Intentions?

As you start thinking about the parenting intentions that you would like to carry with you, I want you to think hard about the role your past could play in the intentions process—that is, whether your parenting intentions are being *dictated* or *influenced* by your childhood.

All would-be parents have ideas about the kind of parent they want to be for their child. Those ideas don't appear out of nowhere—we get them from the examples of friends and family, from parenting books, from social media, and yes, from things we experienced as children.

Just like we discussed back in chapter 1, being *influenced* by your past means simply drawing lessons from it, while having it *dictate* your intentions means taking your past as an exact model (either to follow or to avoid). When your parenting intentions are dictated by your childhood, you will focus on your experience and the way it made you feel, rather than focusing on your child's unique needs and personality.

If you're not entirely sure of the difference, the following questions can help you determine whether your parenting intentions are being dictated by your past.

1. **Are you trying to fix a negative core belief you have about yourself?** No matter how good your intention is or how consistently you fulfill it, it will not prove to you that you're good enough, lovable, or whatever else your negative core belief tells you you're not. Those wounds need to be healed outside of parenting.

2. **Are you flexible with your intentions changing over time?** As your child grows older, your parenting intentions will need to change to meet their new stage of life. If you can't handle the thought of your intention changing, it may be because your past is dictating it.

3. **Are your intentions realistic and achievable?** An intention like *I always want to be calm when helping my children* sets

you up for disappointment. Nothing kills a good parenting intention like expecting perfect performance.

With this in mind, I invite you to explore your own parenting intentions. The next two activities will help you get started.

Activity 8.1
Setting Your Intentions

To help you begin to set parenting intentions, it can help to separate the two key components that make up a parenting intention:

1. The characteristics or emotions you'd like to portray through your parenting

2. The behaviors you want to embody

First, think about the characteristics or emotions you'd like to portray through your parenting—what you'd like to provide to or model for your child—and write these down in the first column of the table provided. Parenting characteristics are pretty easy for most parents to choose. They might include curiosity, kindness, support, patience, flexibility, consistency, and dependability. Emotions are a bit trickier; while none of them are inherently good or bad, some are more uncomfortable than others, especially if they're associated with problematic behavior. Still, I don't recommend setting an intention to only show the "good" emotions in your parenting. It's healthy for your children to see you experience and appropriately express a range of emotions, including frustration, fear, embarrassment, and guilt. Calmly sharing these feelings (e.g., "When I saw you run into the street, I got really angry—I was frustrated that you didn't listen when I told you to stop, and I was afraid you would get hurt") can lead to important conversations that help the child modify their behavior or express their emotions in a more appropriate way.

Next, in the second column of the table, list the behaviors you want to exhibit as a parent. Putting your desired characteristics or emotions into action is how you build connection with your child and foster their growth. Some behaviors I recommend are showing respect, listening to understand, providing boundaries, setting limits, and apologizing. Write down the behaviors that will help you embody your values and model them for your child.

To help with your brainstorming, I've included a list in the appendix with more examples of characteristics, behaviors, and emotions.

Characteristics and Emotions	Behaviors

Now it's time to put these pieces together to create your parenting intentions. You will be writing your intentions using this format:

I want to be [*characteristic or emotion you'd like to embody*] by [*how you behaviorally plan to show the characteristic*].

Write down three intentions that you would like to start implementing, based on the values you've listed and the behaviors that will allow you to embody each value. Remember that it's okay if your intentions are influenced by your past, but they should not be dictated by it. You want to focus on your child's needs, not yours.

1. I want to be _____

   by _____

2. I want to be _____

   by _____

3. I want to be _____

   by _____

If you find yourself struggling to create your parenting intentions, you aren't alone. Many parents spend weeks identifying their intentions. The following activity will guide you through the next step in this process: looking more closely at your child's specific needs to set intentions for parenting in the present.

Activity 8.2
Parenting in the Present

To further clarify your parenting intentions—and begin parenting in the present—practice taking time to consider what your child needs from you in this moment. This can be tricky to figure out, but asking yourself this question can help: "Does my child need me to listen to them, protect them, comfort them, or play with them?" If you aren't sure, you can also ask them! Children are very honest and will tell you exactly what they need.

Once you identify what your child currently needs from you, brainstorm some characteristics or emotions that you think would best support their need, and write these down in the first column of the table provided. For example, if your child is upset because their screen time limit is up, perhaps they need your compassion and empathy so they can better navigate their disappointment. Or if your child is being overly intrusive because they've been independently playing for most of the afternoon, they are likely bored and could benefit from some creativity and stimulation.

Next, identify the behaviors you want to adopt in order to embody these emotions and characteristics, and write these down in the second column. Remember that these behaviors should be observable actions that someone can *see* you do. For example, if your child is upset and needs compassion, you could sit quietly with them, hug them, or rock them in your arms. Or if they are bored and need stimulation, you could give them choices for a joint activity and then play with them. When selecting these behaviors, remember that children model everything! If you yell, "Calm down!" expect the opposite to happen. Show the behavior you are hoping to see your child engage in.

As you make your list, if you need more examples of characteristics, emotions, or behaviors, see the list in the appendix.

Characteristics and Emotions	Behaviors

As you continue to practice identifying and meeting your child's needs, you may discover that you need to revise or expand your list of parenting intentions from activity 8.1. Remember to structure each new intention in this way: "I want to be [*characteristic or emotion you'd like to embody*] by [*how you behaviorally plan to show the characteristic*]."

At this point, you should have a solid working draft of your parenting intentions. But remember: None of these intentions are meant to be exhaustive or final. Your parenting intentions can change every day! In fact, you will need to adapt your intentions frequently based on your child's needs, stage of life, and current challenges.

Parenting intentions help lay the foundation for no longer parenting the child you were but instead raising the child you have. These intentions are not designed to focus on your own needs, even though they involve your behaviors and emotions. This is because you only have control over your own emotions and actions, but it is your actions that will meet your child's needs. Like every role you have in your life, parenting consists of thoughts, decisions, reactions, and assumptions. Each of these aspects will influence your parenting intentions and vice versa. The next step in parenting the child you have is monitoring and correcting the thoughts, decisions, reactions, and assumptions you hold about your child and their behaviors.

Chapter 9

Assumptions, Comparisons, and Labels . . . Oh My!

"Why is my child acting like that?"

"He needs to be disciplined more."

"I know we raised her better than that."

"Why are they so manipulative?"

"Why can't he be more like his brother?"

"She's spoiled."

These are only some of the many thoughts I hear parents share about their children. When a distressing event or undesirable behavior occurs, it's only natural to have some negative thoughts in response. As you might recall from chapter 1, the human brain tries to fit current situations into themes from the past. For example, if you have childhood memories of being ignored, your automatic thought when your child doesn't acknowledge you may be "He's ignoring me," rather than "Maybe he's preoccupied with something." Then there are the emotions that these thoughts trigger. The thought "He's ignoring me" may bring up feelings of being disrespected, unloved, or unappreciated, prompting you to "prove" that you are respected loved, or appreciated. To parent the child you have, you need to actively monitor, challenge, and replace the automatic thoughts and emotions you have about your child, yourself, and your relationship.

Monitoring Your Thoughts About Your Child

The average person has over six thousand thoughts a day (Tseng & Poppenk, 2020), not including what the subconscious contributes. Add in the fact that every time your child engages in a behavior, your mind is giving it meaning (likely one based on your childhood experiences), and . . . well, that's a lot to think about.

Every parent has thoughts and assumptions about their child's behaviors. Regardless of whether your child listens to every direction given or appears to have "lost their damn mind" (yes, I hear that one a lot), you're constantly trying to understand and interpret why your child is doing what they're doing. Monitoring these thoughts is a crucial aspect of parenting the child you have. First, if the automatic thoughts you have about your child's behavior are negative or accusatory, you're more likely to leave your window of tolerance and resort to one of the parenting styles identified in chapter 2. Second, thoughts occur within a matter of seconds, so if you don't challenge them, they are likely to be stored in your brain for future reference. For example, the thought that your toddler is manipulative or attention-seeking is likely to come up again, especially when they're fifteen and pushing back against your rules.

You cannot meet your child's needs when your assumptions about them are inaccurate. Therefore, parenting the child you have requires actively monitoring the automatic thoughts you have about your child, yourself, and your relationship. By learning to slow your thoughts and identify what they're telling you, you'll be able to challenge them and replace them with thoughts that help you understand how your child is feeling and why.

There are three main types of thoughts that need to be actively monitored: assumptions, comparisons, and labels.

Assumptions

Assumptions are thoughts that you believe without any proof. Surprisingly, both negative *and* positive assumptions can hinder you in parenting the child you have.

The main problem with negative assumptions is that they can easily become self-fulfilling prophecies. One father told me that he's strict with his daughters because, in his words, "I was a teenage boy once, and I'm not letting my kids stay out late and get in trouble." A month later, his daughter called him for a ride home from a party where she had been drinking. His prohibitive parenting, driven by an assumption based on his own past, contributed to his child lashing out and engaging in inappropriate behaviors.

Negative assumptions also make it easier to respond disproportionately to your child's behavior. If your child is screaming while you're trying to leave the house, you may assume she's screaming in order to get attention or manipulate you. In fact, she may be overwhelmed because she can't find her shoes and needs to be reassured that you won't leave without her.

On the other side of the coin, positive assumptions can also get in the way of effective parenting. While it may seem like a great alternative to always assume the best about your child, it can sometimes allow children to avoid being held accountable for harmful actions, making the behavior likely to continue or escalate. One couple who brought their seven-year-old son for therapy shared that when he was playing with his younger sister, he pushed her down. However, the parents added, "We don't think he meant it. It was probably an accident." A week later, the school started calling to report similar acting-out behavior.

Ignoring undesirable behavior will not only cause you to miss your child's unmet needs, but it can also lower your child's self-esteem. For example, if you assume your child did their best but they know they didn't, they may think you don't believe they are capable of more. I once had a conversation with a sixteen-year-old girl and her dad in which the daughter expressed frustration about her latest math exam grade. Her dad interjected, "Well, you did your best." To his surprise, the daughter teared up and snapped, "You think a C+ is my best? How dumb do you think I am?"

The bottom line is that you shouldn't assume the best or the worst. The only assumption you should be making about your child or their behavior is that you're missing information. When you know you're missing information, it allows you to enter a conversation or situation with the belief that you need to gather more knowledge about your child, not immediately jump into disciplining or coddling them. Most of the time, you'll find that your child's undesirable behavior is a reflection of something else going on in their life. When you set your assumptions aside, you can engage with your child to identify the "why" behind their behavior and teach them how to appropriately express their emotions.

Activity 9.1
Monitoring and Challenging Assumptions

This activity will get you into the habit of identifying and challenging the automatic thoughts you have about your child and their behaviors. The next time your child starts to show undesirable behaviors or difficult emotions, answer the following questions.

1. What is the behavior?

2. What about your child's behavior upsets you?

3. What were they doing immediately before they engaged in the behavior that could be contributing to it (e.g., having a bad day at school, losing a soccer game)? List as many ideas as you can.

4. Why do you think they engaged in the behavior?

_____

_____

_____

5. What emotions are they exhibiting?

_____

_____

_____

6. Why do you think they are exhibiting those emotions?

_____

_____

_____

7. What are some other possible reasons why your child engaged in the initial behavior?

_____

_____

_____

8. How might your past be impacting how you view your child and their current behavior?

_____

_____

_____

Comparisons and Labels

Labels involve classifying your child within a specific category, whether it's something you see as negative (e.g., stubborn, rude, selfish) or positive (e.g., easygoing, smart, responsible). Comparisons involve pointing out similarities or differences between your child and another person, typically siblings ("Why can't you be more like your sister?"), other children ("You kids today are lazy and entitled!"), or their parents when they were children ("You are just like your father!").

The labels and comparisons you make are largely rooted in your own past experiences or unmet needs, and they are often focused on the generation you grew up in or how you wished you had been characterized as a child. But whether the comparison is "My generation has a stronger work ethic" or "I wish I was as talented as you are," it's unfair to dictate your child's actions based on how you were expected to behave or what you wish you'd done.

Have you ever heard the old saying "Comparison is the thief of joy"? It is especially true in your relationship with your children. Parents frequently label or compare their child in an effort to motivate them ("Your sister doesn't act like this—please act your age") or boost their confidence ("You're the best player on the soccer team"), but whether it's meant as a compliment or an insult, it can have damaging effects on your child.

First, it diminishes your child to a behavior or action, rather than acknowledging them as a whole person. Remember, your words become your child's eternal thoughts—your child will hear this label in their mind for their entire life, making it almost impossible to work their way out of it. Second, children typically attempt to reach the standard you set for them. If you give your child the label *genius* or *best athlete*, they will feel immense pressure to live up to that label in an effort to make you proud. When they don't fulfill that positive label, it will negatively impact their self-esteem. On the other hand, if your comparisons or labels are negative, your child will pull away from you to avoid those comments. Not only will it not make your child work harder, but your negative label may also become a self-fulfilling prophecy. *If you already think I'm bad*, the logic goes, *I'll show you how bad I can be.*

Labeling a child's behaviors, rather than recognizing their effort, can easily cause them to develop a fixed mindset, believing that their abilities and traits cannot be changed, regardless of their determination or effort. I recently heard a family friend discuss how "naturally smart" her daughter was. About a month later, she called me for advice because her daughter had stopped studying—being naturally smart obviously meant she didn't need to! This child needed her mother to help her develop a growth mindset, which is based on the belief that while we each have a different starting point in life, we all have the potential to learn, change, and cultivate our basic qualities (such as intelligence) through our efforts and the support we receive from others (Dweck, 2016).

Finally, labeling and comparing your child teaches them to label and compare themselves. This fosters resentment against you and their siblings and even destroys your child's relationship with themselves, setting them up for a future full of competition, criticism, and negative core beliefs. For you as the parent, seeing the negative consequences of labeling your child will impact how you feel about yourself, increasing your own negative core beliefs.

Activity 9.2
Monitoring Labels and Comparisons

This activity will help you identify the labels you may have inadvertently been using while parenting and brainstorm alternative phrases you can use to foster a growth mindset. You will also reflect on the ways you compare your child to others, what you hope to achieve by making those comparisons, and how you can reframe your thoughts to better appreciate and support your child as a unique individual. I recommend repeating this exercise several times, exploring all the labels and comparisons that come to mind when you think about your child.

Labels

1. Identify a *positive* label you have recently used to describe your child or their behavior.

2. How might your child be negatively impacted by this label?

3. What are some alternative phrases to this label that would reflect a growth mindset?

4. Identify a *negative* label you have recently used to describe your child or their behavior.

_____

_____

_____

5. How might your child be negatively impacted by this label?

_____

_____

_____

6. What are some alternative phrases to this label that would reflect a growth mindset?

_____

_____

_____

Comparisons

1. Whom are you comparing your child to, and what action are you hoping they will engage in?

_____

_____

_____

2. What would you think about yourself, as a parent, if your child behaved the way you want them to?

3. How might your child be negatively impacted by this comparison?

4. How might you describe this aspect of your child—whether it's a strength, a challenge, or a behavior—without comparing them to others?

Instead of Assumptions, Labels, and Comparisons, Try Communication

While it may seem like unoriginal advice, parenting the child you have requires you to communicate with them. It can be difficult for parents to get enough quality communication time with their children, between heavy workloads, hectic schedules, and those pesky smartphone screens. To understand your child on a deeper level, it is important to learn how to communicate effectively with them by shifting how you respond when your child is having a difficult time or showing big emotions. Certain phrases are more useful than others, and trading out accusatory phrases for softer, gentler language can go a long way in helping your child open up, as the following paragraphs will demonstrate. These phrases will help you begin to correct the thoughts you have about your child. But remember that it isn't only *what* you say, but *how* you say it—critical or harsh tones can rapidly cause a child to shut down.

"How Come?"

Regardless of how caring your tone might be, the word *why* has a way of making others feel instantly defensive or fearful. The next time someone asks you a *why* question, notice how you feel. Questions like "Why are you wearing that?" or "Why didn't you call?" convey the message that no answer will satisfy the person asking it.

To understand who your child is, how they think, and what they are feeling, trade the *why* for *how come*. I can't explain why the brain interprets these two phrases so differently, but it does. "How come you are wearing that?" or "How come you didn't call?" sound genuinely curious and inviting, rather than accusatory or judgmental. For the next couple of days, practice replacing *why* with *how come* when talking to your child (followed by sincerely listening to their answer) and note how differently they respond to you.

"I See . . ."

This phrase works really well with both toddlers and teenagers. State "I see . . ." and then identify the emotion or experience you're observing— for example, "I see you're happy" or "I see you're scared." It may feel strange at first to state what seems obvious, but this allows your child to confirm or correct your statement, opening the door for conversation and connection. It also shows your child that you see them! It's okay if you get the emotion wrong or your child turns away in embarrassment or anger. The point is to let them know that you see them and aren't trying to fix or change them.

"What Do You Think About What Happened?"

When your child experiences a significant event or life circumstance, especially a difficult one, it can be easy to assume what they are thinking or feeling about it. However, these assumptions result in missed opportunities to learn about your child. You might assume your child is sad after they lose a basketball game, but perhaps they're thrilled that they came so close to beating the state champions; assuming they're sad will only teach them to second-guess the positive emotions they're feeling. Similarly, you might assume your child is happy about being asked to a dance, but if they're actually disappointed that they weren't asked by the person they like, assuming they're happy because they at least got asked by someone may close down the conversation before it ever gets started.

Some parents struggle to ask about their child's experiences because they don't know how to manage their child's uncomfortable emotions; they want their child to focus on the positive side of things, rather than sulk in misery. But these are vital opportunities to connect with your child, learn about how they perceive what's happening to them, and teach them how to cope with their emotions. Instead of pushing challenging experiences aside, you and your child can come together as a team to handle the event.

"I Wonder What's Happening"

To avoid missing information about what your child is going through, I recommend the following phrase: "I wonder what's happening." Since this remark isn't a question, it doesn't make your child feel like they need to have the "right" answer. In fact, I've found that using this phrase in a curious tone, within earshot of your child, often prompts them to voluntarily share what they are experiencing with you.

"I Wonder What You (They) Are Needing"

When your child is going through a difficult situation, it's vital to ask them what they believe they need. This phrase lets your child know that you want and are able to meet their needs. It also gives them time to think about the question before answering. You can ask the question directly to your child if they're in their window of tolerance or say, "I wonder what they are needing" to yourself or your partner while your child is close by. If your child is unable to answer (either respectfully or at all), let them know that whenever they feel ready, you're willing to talk about it and help in any way you can.

"How Would You Like to Make Things Better?"

This is a great question, but only when it's used at the right time. When a child is actively upset, they won't be able to think logically enough to consider the consequences of their behavior. But once your child is back in their window—able to give and receive information and stay emotionally regulated—this question can help your child think about a variety of solutions to rectify their behavior.

"How Would You Like Things to Be Different in the Future?"

Sometimes making something better in the moment isn't possible. Whether your child experienced a life struggle (such as failing a class or getting sick and missing a big event) or made a mistake (like breaking curfew or being caught in a lie), helping them think about what they would like to change in the future is an opportunity to learn about your child while encouraging their problem-solving skills. It also helps your child recognize that they have control of their actions and the repercussions.

"What Do You Think About . . . ?"

Try asking your child how they view themselves—for instance, "How do you think you did studying for your test?" or "What do you think about your behavior with your brother?"—before interjecting your own thoughts and opinions. Allowing your child to honestly assess their intentions and behaviors will help you understand and connect with your child, while also helping them learn to change their behavior themselves in order to achieve their own goals.

Acknowledge Their Feelings

Children tend to be either really proud or really disappointed about the outcome of a situation or event. Acknowledging those feelings, instead of trying to fix or correct them, will help your child process their emotions and acknowledge their own efforts. Phrases like "You seem really proud of your hard work!" or "You seem disappointed that you didn't get picked for the team" allow your child to share their feelings in a safe way without fear of you labeling them, criticizing them, or trying to change their feelings by "fixing" the situation.

Recognize Their Actions

A growth mindset is characterized by the ability to change and enhance parts of yourself, but the only way to develop this mindset is to recognize the effort you are putting forth. That's why one of my favorite recommendations for parents is to recognize your child's efforts along with their accomplishments and behaviors. "I saw you studying really hard," "I know you've been juggling a lot of responsibilities," and "I really appreciate your effort in cleaning your room" all tell your child that you see, appreciate, and believe in their ability to grow and change for the better.

Learning to Adjust Your Approach

When a distressing event or undesirable behavior occurs, it's only natural to have some negative thoughts in response. However, the simple act of monitoring your thoughts in these moments can have a profound impact on your relationship with your child. If you can adjust your approach from accusations and assumptions to curiosity and communication, you can turn your negative thoughts into opportunities to strengthen your connection with your child.

And communication isn't just for the challenging moments. Just like any relationship, your relationship with your child gets stronger with every effort you make to understand, accept, and appreciate them for who they are. It has the added benefit of teaching your child how to be curious about others. Remember, modeling the behaviors you'd like to see in your child makes the greatest impact.

Chapter 10

Identifying Your Expectations

All relationships are full of expectations, and parenting is no exception. From the moment you decided to have a child, you likely started imagining what kind of child you were going to have, including their behaviors, interests, future career, and more. Within those hopes and desires, your expectations started taking form.

An expectation is any strongly held belief that something will happen or eventually be true in the future. Expectations typically form for three different reasons:

1. **If you have unmet needs or desires from the past, you may expect that your relationship with your child will meet those needs or fulfill those desires.** For example, if you expect your child to clean their room or do their chores, what are you getting out of it? A clean house? Proof that your child listens to you and respects your home? Not having to smell or stare at a pile of dirty clothes? With every expectation you have, there is always something you are getting out of it. But if

your expectations are being dictated by the past, you won't be able to parent the child you have.

2. **You may create expectations to help your child avoid a hardship or obstacle you've dealt with.** This may look like expecting your child to complete their homework because you struggled to get into college and don't want them to experience the same trials. Almost every parent I've seen wants their child to be "better" than they were or have an easier life. Parents create expectations for their children in the hope that it will help them get ahead, but in the end, it's really your needs being met when these expectations are fulfilled.

3. **Your expectations mirror the expectations your parents had for you in childhood.** If your parents expected you to have dinner with them every night, you will likely expect your child to do the same. But even "good" expectations can diminish your relationship with your child when they are not created or communicated effectively. These inherited expectations tend to be so ingrained that you might not even be fully aware of what they are—you just know when they're not met.

Expectations aren't necessarily a bad thing. But even expectations that are meant to help your child can cause them to miss out on their own unique experiences and learning opportunities.

First of all, if expectations are not developmentally appropriate, clearly articulated to your child, and—above all—flexible, they can create serious challenges in your relationship. And it should go without saying that having too many expectations within any relationship creates unnecessary pressure, which in turn creates hostility. Your child wants a loving relationship with you, one in which they know that if (and when) they don't meet your expectations, you'll still welcome them with open arms. Just think of a time when your parent held you to an expectation, one that they weren't willing to modify or even discuss with you. Did it cause you to feel closer to them, or pull away? Did you fear what they would think about you if you failed? Did you resent them for not listening to what you need? The majority of the children I work with answer yes to at least one of those questions. They want their parents to listen and talk about the expectations given to them.

Second, expectations create a debt-debtor relationship in which unconditional love becomes (or seems to become) conditional. When you place an expectation onto your child, what they hear is, "I'll love you *if* you _____." Children often feel that to be loved by their parents, they must meet or exceed the standards being given to them. When I ask children how they feel about these standards, they respond, "It's crushing me; I am doing the best I can," "I wish they understood how bad it makes me feel," and "I know I'm not the kid they want." A loving parent-child relationship shouldn't include an array of standards for the child to live up to.

Finally, the biggest challenge with expectations is that when they aren't met, it can lead some parents to control or coerce their child. They may insist that their way is the best way and throw even more expectations at their child. For example, parents who hold the expectation that their child receive straight A's in school may punish the child for lower grades or try to bribe their child with money for every A they receive. Not only is this a fast way to ruin your relationship, but it also breaks down your communication.

Some parents push back at the concept of changing or removing their expectations, fearing their child will drop out of school, behave recklessly, or otherwise jeopardize their goals (or the parent's goals for them). In fact, the topic of expectations brings more pushback and puzzled looks from parents than any other one I teach. "Everyone needs to have expectations, Dr. Brie," said one dad. "My boss, society, and the world have expectations of me."

"What happens if you don't meet those expectations because you have personal issues going on?" I asked.

"I'd probably get fired," he replied.

"And is that the type of relationship you want with your child?" I asked him. "The type of relationship where if your child doesn't live up to your standard, they receive consequences, regardless of what was going on with them?"

I'm not suggesting that we should live in a world without consequences. But because your child hasn't been alive as long as you have, it's your job as their parent to love, educate, and guide—in that exact order. That's why I recommend that you co-create expectations with your child that are based on their needs and developmentally appropriate.

With that in mind, I encourage you to read the rest of this chapter thoroughly, and experiment with a few of the recommendations, before shutting down or moving on. Challenging and recreating your expectations is vital to parenting the child you have.

Activity 10.1

Identifying Your Expectations

When co-creating expectations with your child, the first order of business is—you guessed it—identifying where your expectations are coming from. Parenting the child you have means discarding expectations that are dictated by your past unmet needs, the challenges you went through, or how your parents expected you to behave. To do so, start by describing an expectation you have for your child. Then think about what it would say about you and your child if the expectation were met and, with this knowledge, try to identify where the expectation came from.

Here is an example to help you get started:

Expectation: *I expect my child to do their best in school.*

What would it say about your child if they accomplished this expectation? *That they are hardworking, smart, dedicated, and going to have a better life.*

What would it say about you as a parent if your child accomplished this expectation? *That I'm a great parent who raised hardworking kids.*

Where does this expectation come from? *My parents never really pushed me to try my best at school, and I struggled to learn those habits. I don't want my kids to have the same problem.*

Now it's your turn:

1. Expectation #1: _____

   _____

   What would it say about your child if they accomplished this expectation?

   _____

   _____

   _____

What would it say about you as a parent if your child accomplished this expectation?

_____

_____

_____

Where does this expectation come from?

_____

_____

_____

2. Expectation #2: _____

_____

What would it say about your child if they accomplished this expectation?

_____

_____

_____

What would it say about you as a parent if your child accomplished this expectation?

_____

_____

_____

Where does this expectation come from?

3. Expectation #3: _____

What would it say about your child if they accomplished this expectation?

What would it say about you as a parent if your child accomplished this expectation?

Where does this expectation come from?

Characteristics of Appropriate Expectations

The next thing to consider is whether your expectations are developmentally appropriate for your child. Are they concise? Are they flexible? Have they been clearly communicated? Many parents' expectations start out too advanced or too detailed. The following are important factors to consider in co-creating expectations with your child.

The first thing to consider is the intensity and the duration of the expectation you're setting—how challenging will it be for your child, and how much time is it likely to take? If your expectations are not age-appropriate for your child, they will respond in one of two ways: shutting down before they even begin or exhausting themselves in the attempt to complete it. For example, imagine you've told your seven-year-old that they need to clean their incredibly dirty room before playing outside. Many children will immediately leave their window of tolerance because the task feels so overwhelming. Some children won't even start or, at best, they will do a half-baked job and hope you don't notice. Other children, especially those who are oriented toward people-pleasing, will do everything they can to complete the task but run out of time to play.

Remember that children spend most of their lives building their self-worth through their external achievements. Unrealistic, developmentally inappropriate expectations can actually harm children because it sets them up to go through life believing that if they were only smart enough or tried harder, they could achieve these things. If you're looking for guidance on how to set age-appropriate expectations, there are many resources online that break recommendations down by task or chore. One place to start would be the American

Academy of Child and Adolescent Psychiatry: https://www.aacap
.org/AACAP/Families_and_Youth/Facts_for_Families/FFF-Guide
/Chores_and_Children-125.aspx. My professional recommendation is
to limit a task to no more than four minutes per age of your child,
beginning at age five. For example, a five-year-old can complete a four-
minute chore, while a ten-year-old can complete a forty-minute chore.

In addition to being developmentally appropriate, expectations
should be precise and specific, rather than vague and nonstop. This
allows everyone to understand the requirement and provides achievable
starting and finishing points. The expectation most commonly shared
in my therapy room is the one I hate the most: expecting a child to *do
their best.* It simply leaves too much room for interpretation, making
it a lot easier for your child to fall short of what you had in mind.
Instead, talk with your child about the expectations they have for
themselves and how they would like to achieve those expectations. You
can also share your expectation, but highlight the effort you hope to
see, rather than the outcome.

Expectations should also be flexible. Many children today have a
wide range of interests, priorities, and responsibilities. It's important
for parents to be understanding when things arise that conflict
with their expectations. Imagine that your son's soccer team made
the playoffs, but he has a math test the same day. Requiring him to
practice soccer *and* study for two hours isn't going to be healthy for
him. Instead, talk with your child to identify the area he most needs
to focus on, and alter the expectation. Co-creating a new expectation
will teach your child time management skills that help him balance
numerous responsibilities.

Finally, appropriate expectations must be clearly communicated
between you, your child, and your partner. You'd be surprised how
many parents have expectations for their children that they've never

mentioned, either to the child or to the other parent. Having family meetings in which you all discuss the events and priorities of the week is a good way to start co-creating expectations together. During this time, you can also discuss potential consequences and rewards for the outcome of the expectations. Including your partner in the conversation will help prevent your child from playing you against each other with the classic "I'll go ask the other parent instead" move.

Co-creating Expectations with Your Child

As you've learned, expecting your child to live by another person's expectations rarely has positive effects. However, co-creating expectations with your child—that is, helping your child learn how to identify their *own* expectations and then live by those standards— can have long-lasting benefits. If you'd like your child to learn who they are, rather than pressuring them to live up to expectations that were likely passed down from previous generations, then discussing expectations should begin early in your child's life.

This can begin as early as six to seven years of age, when children can start to think about the type of person they want to be. A good way to start is to ask your child about people they like or admire: "What do you like about that person? What traits do they have that you would like to develop?" Common answers include *strong, good, caring,* and *helpful,* while older children may answer *hardworking, rich, loyal,* and *brave.* If your child answers with an unrealistic person or trait (such as a superhero), try to avoid pointing out their error. Instead, ask them how that person treats other people, or point out a few behaviors you saw the person do (e.g., using their powers to rescue people who were in danger).

After you've talked with your child about the people they like and the qualities they would like to develop, you can begin helping them think about how they would like to develop those qualities in themselves. Be careful not to push them toward doing it the way *you* think such qualities should be developed. If you had the desire to become a nicer person but someone was directing you how to do it, it could turn you away from ever trying to be nice again! Here are some questions I recommend asking your child:

- How would you like to become more [*characteristic*]?

- Would you like help becoming [*characteristic*]? If so, how?

- If [*pet's name*] were to follow you around and see you being [*characteristic*], what would they see you do?

- How would you like to develop [*characteristic*] at school, at home, on the sports field, and so forth?

If you continue these conversations as your child ages, you'll be able to help them develop, refine, and strengthen their own standards.

What Expectations Does Your Child Have for You?

When you started this chapter, you probably didn't think we'd discuss the expectations your child has for you. I admit it's unusual for a book on parenting, but if we're discussing understanding your child's needs, it's something that must be considered.

When I was growing up, I rarely expected both of my parents to be home for dinner. But if someone had asked me what I *needed*, I would definitely have mentioned needing family dinners at least three nights a week. I needed consistency, predictability, and to know that I was important to my parents—and in my mind, I would have received all those things if we had family dinners together.

However, children are often told that they shouldn't expect anything from their parents because they aren't in charge, they don't make the rules, and they don't have as many responsibilities as their parents. But just as you might attempt to get your needs met by placing expectations on your child, your child will attempt to get their needs met by setting expectations for you. While I'm not advocating that you bend over backward at every request your child makes, you should be open to hearing what they expect and then ask why (or maybe *how come*) that expectation is important to them. The information you gain from the request can give you a lot of insight into your child.

For example, eleven-year-old Aaliyah had busy parents who frequently ordered out due to their work schedules. She shared her expectation that her parents not only cook dinner at least four nights a week, but also teach her how to make at least one of those meals. When asked how come it was important to her to learn how to cook, Aaliyah answered, "It would be time that I would get to spend with them." Behind Aaliyah's expectation was a need for more individual attention and bonding with her parents—she just didn't know how to ask for it. After understanding this, Aaliyah's parents made an extra effort to sit down with her and talk about her day when they got home from work. They even managed to cook together a bit more often.

During your next family meeting, try asking your child to list five to ten expectations they have for you and why those things are important to them. My guess is that you'll see a common theme that reveals what your child really needs from you.

Try Out a New Tradition

Many parents struggle with this chapter, and I'll admit that these ideas are quite a bit different from traditional parenting. But let's remember that traditional parenting often means parenting the child you were, not the child you have. Co-creating expectations is a way of increasing your communication with your child, allowing you to learn more about who you're raising and giving you the chance to openly discuss the values and beliefs you would like to pass on to them.

Chapter 11

Decisions, Responses, and Apologies

I recently heard a statistic that the average parent makes over one thousand decisions a day. (No wonder you're exhausted by mid-morning!) From feeding your child breakfast to tucking them into bed, you make hundreds of choices that impact your children—and, if you're like most of the parents I see, you probably lie in bed at night ruminating over every one. *Did I make the right choice? Will it land them in therapy? Will they be scarred for life?* This late-night second-guessing is even harder when you consider how many of those decisions happen within a split second. Sometimes you may not even know why you're making a certain choice or responding a certain way.

Now I'm not saying that you have to analyze the hundreds of choices you make each day. But I am encouraging you to slow down your decision-making process. As we've already talked about, identifying the *why* behind your decisions is important for recognizing whose needs are being met by each choice and what outcomes you're hoping for. Slowing down will help you make fewer impulsive decisions, which means fewer regrets at the end of the day. It will also give you an opportunity to align your decisions with the parenting intentions you've set.

Whose Needs Are Being Met?

Many of the choices we make on a daily basis are "selfish"—that is, we choose what we choose because we believe we'll get something out of it. Why do you get out of bed and go to work? To make money so you can pay for things you need and want. Why do you eat the food you eat? Sometimes because it's tasty; sometimes because it will help you lose weight. Even the kindest, most selfless acts—donating money, doing volunteer work, helping out a friend—tend to leave us feeling good about ourselves.

I don't believe making decisions that personally benefit us makes us egotistical; I think it's a natural motivation to behave this way. Unfortunately, though, making parenting decisions based on how *you* will benefit can sometimes hinder you from meeting your child's needs. It's easy to think you're making a choice for your child when, in reality, it's all about what you get out of it.

For example, Mina and Jake brought their nine-year-old son, Andy, to therapy because of challenges at home. "He rarely helps out," Mina explained. "He seems so entitled and lazy."

"Well, he's an only child, and we make good money," Jake responded. "I want him to be happy."

When I asked about smaller parenting decisions, such as who decides what they have for dinner, Mina said they typically let Andy decide. "As long as it is healthy and appropriate, we make it work," she said.

At first glance, it seemed like Andy's parents were responding to his needs by letting him choose the family dinner. But when I asked them what difference that parenting decision made for them, the root desire came out. Mina, who grew up with a mother who never let the kids have input on daily decisions, explained that it made her feel like a good mom because she was giving her son a voice. But by parenting the child she was, not the child she had, Mina had opened the door for Andy to start making other decisions, like refusing to help out at home.

In turn, Mina and Jake realized that what Andy really needed was to learn that he didn't get to make every decision in the home. But, Jake asked, what if they truly didn't care what they had for dinner and wanted Andy to have the choice?

"Letting Andy make the decision likely meets your needs by taking something off your plate," I agreed. "But meeting Andy's need for learning how to follow his parents' directions and go with the flow should be what happens most of the time."

Parenting is a balancing act. I don't expect any parent to meet their child's needs 100 percent of the time—that is impossible, and trying will lead to frustration and exhaustion. There will be times for flexibility and spontaneity, as well as occasions when your needs may need to come first; after all, you can't pour from an empty cup. The key is trying to meet your child's needs first and most often.

Activity 11.1
Identifying Whose Needs Are Being Met

Whenever you're making a parenting decision, it's crucial to identify whose needs are being met in that moment. Are you focused on meeting your child's needs, or are you trying to satisfy your own past needs? To answer this question, it can help to ask yourself, *What difference would this decision make?* You might recognize this pesky question from previous chapters and activities, as it can quickly help identify whose needs are at the forefront of the situation or decision.

1. What was the triggering event?

   Example: *My child got out of bed for the third time that night.*

2. What decision did you make in response to this event?

   Example: *I took my child back to bed and told her if she got out of bed, she'd lose privileges the next day.*

3. What difference does your decision make for your child?

   Example: *My child is able to get her sleep. She learns to obey me. She'll learn to self-soothe.*

4. What difference does your decision make for you?

   Example: *I'm able to enjoy the rest of the quiet evening with my spouse and relax.*

5. What needs do you think your child had during the event that weren't being met?

   Example: *Possibly the need to self-soothe and know that she's safe.*

6. Whose needs do you believe are primarily being met with your decision?

    Example: *Honestly, mostly mine. My child does need sleep, but I'm beat and need some alone time.*

    _____

    _____

    _____

    _____

7. What are some ways and times that you can meet your own needs so you will be more available to meet your child's needs?

    Example: *Before she gets home from school, I can take thirty minutes to relax. If she does get out of bed, it may be quicker to lie down with her for a bit until she's asleep rather than constantly putting her back into bed.*

    _____

    _____

    _____

    _____

Remember that it's okay if your needs are being met with your decision. However, you'll ideally find other occasions to meet your needs so you can focus on meeting your child's needs with your parenting decisions. If you're struggling to identify what your child needs from you (physical, emotional, and psychological safety, comfort, or belonging), review the examples in activity 1.2.

Decreasing Impulsive Reactions

When you're faced with a decision, do you feel like you need to make your choice right away? You probably don't! In fact, one of the best techniques I teach parents is *waiting* to respond to your child or make a parenting choice.

The situations that require an immediate parenting decision are the ones that prevent serious injury, such as a toddler darting into the street or a teen attempting to run away from home. Other incidents, like your toddler throwing clothes or your teen skipping class, may make you *feel* like you need to respond right away. But few good decisions are made in the minutes after a challenging behavior or situation occurs. When you respond immediately, it usually means you're reacting impulsively—and as we've already learned, knee-jerk responses are usually an attempt to meet your own needs, rather than your child's.

Instead, take time to slow down and think about your response, which will help you align your decision with the parenting intentions you've set. As you'll remember from chapter 8, parenting intentions comprise two components:

1. A characteristic or emotion you'd like to embody

2. A behavior you can use to exhibit that characteristic or emotion

If the characteristic or emotion in your intention isn't available to you because you're out of your window of tolerance, take a break until you are able to access that emotion and choose a behavior that helps you display that characteristic. You want to ensure that your unmet needs don't dictate your reaction.

When slowing down, I also strongly recommend including your child's other parent in the process. For many of my clients, co-parenting is a struggle. But it's important for the two of you to work together to identify what needs your child may have and how you can meet them, together or individually. When discussing the situation with your partner, make sure you are both in your window of tolerance and ready to honestly explore what unmet needs, past traumas, or negative experiences may be triggering you.

For example, Zach and Ali brought their thirteen-year-old daughter, Reagan, into therapy when they discovered she hadn't been completing her schoolwork. The school reported that Reagan was also habitually zoning out and distracting her peers. Zach and Ali wanted to immediately ground Reagan and take her phone away; instead, they chose to hold off until they discussed the situation in therapy the next day.

While in session, Zach and Ali considered what Reagan's behaviors might be triggering for them. Ali shared that she never struggled in school and always wanted to make her parents proud: "I can't imagine not completing my schoolwork when I was her age." Zach mentioned being confused and irritated by Reagan's behavior, noting, "We give her everything, yet she can't do her homework."

Once Ali and Zach returned to their window of tolerance, we reviewed the basic needs for emotional, psychological, and physical safety, comfort, and belonging. This helped them identify several areas in which Reagan could be struggling: "Maybe she's not getting enough time with us individually. Maybe she's struggling with her schoolwork and doesn't know how to ask for help. Or she's having challenges with peers or someone at school. Maybe she's afraid she'll disappoint us."

Later, Ali and Zach took Reagan out and discussed what was happening at school. Reagan admitted that she was being ostracized by her peer group and was preoccupied with trying to make new friends.

By acknowledging their own triggers and unmet needs, Ali and Zach were able to listen and better understand their child's needs.

When I asked Ali and Zach about their parenting intentions, one of Ali's intentions went like this: "I want to be more present and available for my child by putting my phone down and no longer working at home." I asked Ali how she would like to approach Reagan's challenges at school through her parenting intention, and she stated that she would like to start turning off screens at 6 p.m. to spend more time with Reagan, as well as planning "girls' days" with her daughter and one of her friends to help her develop new relationships.

Even when you've taken time to slow down and realign with your parenting intentions, your unmet needs and past negative experiences can still creep into the response you give. You may find yourself either giving advice to your child about how to solve their problem or taking control of the situation to fix it yourself. Again, these are choices that meet your needs, not your child's. Most of the time, children don't want their parents to fix the situation or start giving advice. They simply want the opportunity to share about their experiences and emotions. The next time your child comes to you with a challenge or problem, try asking them this question first: "Would you like me to listen, give advice, or intervene in the situation?"

It's important to actually follow through on your child's request—respect their wishes by only providing the response they've asked for. If they don't ask for your input, you can let them know that if they ever need you to intervene or support them, you're more than happy to help. Your child may eventually ask for your input or assistance, but only after they feel heard and understood.

Apologies (and How to Make Them)

Despite your efforts to slow down the decision-making process and learn how to respond thoughtfully instead of reacting impulsively, there will still be times when you make a parenting decision that doesn't turn out the way you had hoped. The reality is that as a parent, you will make mistakes . . . a lot of them. Once you recognize your missteps, it's very easy to start beating yourself up with all your negative core beliefs, like *I'm not good enough, I'm stupid,* or *I suck at parenting.*

However, mistakes should encourage you—they are evidence that you are trying to change! Instead of trying to be the "perfect parent" and letting your mistakes get the best of you, allow your mistakes to serve as a signal that you simply need to apologize and make repairs. Apologizing doesn't mean admitting that you're a bad parent. Rather, it means you're humble and healthy enough to recognize where you went wrong and how you can improve in the future. There are three steps to correctly apologize to others, specifically your child:

1. Recognize and admit when you make a mistake.

2. State how you would have liked to have handled the situation and what you will try to do in the future.

3. Work on changing your behavior. If an apology occurs but behaviors don't change, it's not a true apology.

Consider the following example. One night, Vivian was making dinner when her daughter, Grace, came to her in tears because she didn't understand her homework. Vivian, who had had a long day, reacted with emotions that she later admitted were completely over the top, and Grace fled the room, even more upset than before. After returning to her window of tolerance, Vivian went to her daughter and deeply apologized for taking her frustration out that way. "I can't imagine how overwhelmed you must feel with your homework," she said, "and I didn't help the situation by yelling. You're allowed to have the emotions you're experiencing. Going back to your homework, would you like me to listen to your frustration, give advice, or intervene?" Grace shared that she felt stupid and feared she would fail her test; she wanted her mother's reassurance and help. After dinner, Vivian helped Grace finish studying and reminded her that her effort and motivation to succeed were more important than the grade she received.

It's Not Always About You

It's hard to not take your child's behaviors personally. After all, you brought them into the world (or into your family) and are attempting to raise them to be a good, happy little human. If they aren't behaving appropriately, it must say something about what you're doing, right?

Not necessarily! Your child is their own separate person with thoughts, ideas, emotions, and experiences that, believe it or not, may have very little to do with you. Assuming that your child's behavior is all about you can lead you to dismiss other things that may be happening in your child's life. For example, Lola, the mother of a six-year-old boy, explained that her son would get very upset whenever she tried to help him get dressed in the morning. "He screams that I'm not doing it right and throws his clothes at me, so I walk out of the room," she shared. Lola was convinced that her son hated her for divorcing his father, and she believed this behavior was her son's way of getting back at her. But when I asked her son why getting dressed caused him so much distress, he simply replied, "I don't like how the clothes feel."

Although it's perfectly normal to assume you play a role in your child's undesirable behaviors, the reality is that you might not. To keep your negative thoughts in line, ask yourself, *What does my child's behavior say about me?* If the answer is one of the core beliefs you stated in chapter 1, your past may be dictating how you parent. If that's the case, you can use all three elements in this chapter to change course: decide to address your unhelpful core belief, slow down your sense of urgency to "get it right," and apologize to yourself for letting an old pattern get in your way. These three internal actions can shift your assumptions into opportunities to heal your past wounds, not to mention heal your relationship with your child while modeling a healthy approach to self-care and personal growth.

Chapter 12

Grieving the Loss of the Child (or Childhood) You Wish You'd Had

Grief is a normal part of everyone's life, from the loss of a family member to the close of a career (even if you've been looking forward to it). Grief can also occur when you feel a deep sense of loss regarding how you experience parenthood, specifically:

1. Grieving the loss of the child you wish you'd had

2. Grieving the loss of the childhood or parent you wish you'd had

Regardless of the type of loss you're experiencing, you deserve for it to be acknowledged, accepted, and healed. As difficult as it can be, healing your grief is absolutely essential for you to parent the child you have.

Wishing You Had a Different Child

When you first became a parent, you may have had several expectations about what your child would be like. Perhaps you envisioned your child playing ball, having tea parties, or following in your career footsteps. But if your child doesn't want to engage in those activities—or, for that matter, if they aren't the gender you were hoping for, or aren't physically or mentally able to live the life you anticipated—it can leave you feeling disappointed, heartbroken, and angry. And denying your grief only makes it come out in ways that cause more harm.

Forcing Activities

Some parents' grief comes out in the form of forcing their children into specific activities and hobbies that they always dreamed of sharing with the child they envisioned. As one teen client shared with me, "I told my mom I didn't want to go out for spirit squad, but she made me. She said that if I didn't, 'there would be consequences.' I think she wants me to be more social . . . but why does it have to be spirit squad?" When I discussed this with the mother, she initially claimed that she wanted her daughter to find a good group of friends and develop a more optimistic attitude. Later, though, she admitted that she'd always dreamed of attending high school football games and watching her daughter cheer on the team. Whether she knew it or not, this mother was wishing for a different type of child while not seeing or hearing the child she had.

We've already talked at length about how not allowing your child a voice in choosing their activities and hobbies can make them feel unheard, leading to resentment or pushback in the present, as well as long-term consequences like struggling to identify their own thoughts and opinions in adulthood. But as you work to identify the root cause of your desire and what unmet needs it may be fulfilling for you, it's important to also feel and acknowledge your own disappointment at not being able to experience things with your child that feel special and important to you.

At the same time, it's crucial that you do not let your child see or experience your disappointment. Most children feel bad after having disappointed a parent, even when it was to some extent intentional (as with defiant words or rebellious actions). However, if a parent shows dissatisfaction regarding their child's personality, interests, or abilities, the child may start feeling bad about who they are. Some children will channel this feeling into withdrawal or rebellion, while others will give up their interests or opinions in order to make the parent happy. As you work on processing your grief, take time alone to journal and think about the emotions you're experiencing. Don't focus on trying to change them—just let them exist and pass on their own.

Shaming Behaviors

In a similar vein, parents grieving the loss of their ideal child may use shaming behaviors to push their child toward a certain career, lifestyle, or even religion. Rather than attempting to understand the emotions or thought process behind their child's choice, the parent may vent their frustration or attempt to achieve the desired outcome with phrases like "You're not going to make any money in that career" or "God would be disappointed in you."

Shaming your child for a bad grade won't encourage them to study harder, any more than shaming them on spiritual or moral grounds will guide them into your beliefs. If anything, shame will only undermine your child's self-worth, causing them to flee further from you and your expectations. Why would they want a relationship with someone who is always disappointed in them? While I have yet to see a child completely mess up their life by choosing certain hobbies, pursuing their own career path, or making occasional mistakes, I have seen a child's life be forever changed—even ended—when their parent shamed or forced them into living the life the parent wanted for them.

If raising your child in a specific spiritual tradition is important to you, there are other ways to engage them spiritually without insisting they attend church or study a sacred text. As we've learned, parenting the child you have involves asking your child to share their own thoughts and ideas about the principles and values that you want to instill. Rather than shaming your child into compliance, practice empathy and curiosity to better understand your child's behaviors. For instance, you could ask, "Considering what you know about our faith, what do you think your behavior reflects about it?"

It can be really hard to watch your child make choices, engage in behaviors, or live a life you don't completely understand. But remember, your child is not an extension of you. They should be allowed to try new things, make mistakes, and have fun adventures without fear that their parent won't love them anymore.

Wishing You Had a Different Childhood (or Parent)

I grew up with a mother who developed and ran a home remodeling business. To call her successful is an understatement. She taught me the importance of hard work, how to be honest and trustworthy, and how to stand up for my values. She also worked seven days a week, and I can't recall one vacation when she wasn't taking work calls or checking emails. Even though my mother taught me so much, I often wish she would have been more present in my childhood.

However, I know other individuals who did have stay-at-home moms and who frequently tell me they wished their parent worked outside of the home or had a passion outside of raising children. No matter what kind of childhood you had, it's entirely normal to wonder what life would have been like with a different type of upbringing, or to think you would have been better off with the opposite of what you had. Whether your parents were physically or psychologically absent or even abusive, you can simultaneously grieve some aspects of your childhood while you appreciate and enjoy other aspects.

The first step in healing grief from your past is to feel every emotion it brings up (such as confusion, anger, sadness, fear, longing, and resentment). While you may want to skim over the pain, this only makes those emotions come out in other ways, such as parenting your child through your past. Because beginning to unpack these emotions can often open the floodgates, so to speak, I recommend journaling through your memories as they come up: events that upset you, choices your parents made, characteristics they displayed. Even positive events that *didn't* happen can be explored. For instance, if you never had a parent tuck you into bed at night, this could create grief and longing for having parents who were present. After describing the event, write down the emotions it brings up as you think about it. Try to stay in your window of tolerance as you journal about these events, taking breaks to self-soothe as needed.

It's possible that you wrote about these events in chapter 5. It's okay (and beneficial) for you to write about them again. I promise, the more you think and write about your painful experiences, the less of an impact they will have on you and your parenting.

The second step is to identify a common theme within these painful memories. Were there one or two primary feelings that these painful experiences left you with? One client I worked with recalled being spanked a lot as a child and was never sure what she did to deserve it. These punishments left her feeling unheard, unimportant, and as though her voice didn't matter to her parents. These themes, if not addressed, can stick with you for decades. In fact, you may notice that they are closely tied with the negative core beliefs you identified in chapter 1.

The final step is to remind yourself of who you are despite how you were raised, or maybe even because of it. For instance, my biological father leaving when I was an infant allowed me to have a stepdad who loved me, raised me, and provided me with a great life that I likely wouldn't have had otherwise. There are some past experiences, such as assault or neglect, that can make it challenging to find any hidden benefits, but they may have offered opportunities for growth. I'm not suggesting that you put a positive spin on your pain or the experiences that caused it, or that the presence of silver linings will justify or excuse another person's abusive behavior. What I am saying is that those experiences can help you develop qualities like perseverance, empathy, and optimism. Grief is a balancing act. If you only look at the negative aspects of your childhood, you won't be able to recognize what those painful experiences taught you or celebrate the new path you are on.

Activity 12.1
Identifying Your Sources of Grief

After you've spent some time journaling about the events and memories that bring up feelings of grief, reflect on the following questions to deepen your exploration of these feelings and their impact on your life.

What themes do you notice within the painful memories you've described in your journal? Were there one or two primary feelings that these experiences left you with? Do you see any overlap between these experiences and the negative core beliefs you identified in activity 1.1?

In what ways have you grown from or been strengthened by these painful experiences? (Remember, this isn't about minimizing others' harmful actions, but acknowledging your own resilience.) Maybe you learned specific skills—like teaching yourself how to cook because your parents didn't prepare your meals—or you developed traits like independence, creativity, and perseverance.

Which aspects of your childhood do you hope your child doesn't experience? What steps have you taken in the hope of preventing these painful experiences—how have you tried to protect your child through your words, actions, and parenting decisions?

Do you think your parenting choices have been effective in ensuring your child won't have similar experiences to your own? Why or why not? Are there any downsides to your approach—any negative effects that you've already noticed or that could become an issue for your child?

_____

_____

_____

_____

_____

_____

The Five Stages of Grief

I've found the five stages of grief to be very useful in working with parents who are grieving their childhood. Developed by psychiatrist Elisabeth Kübler-Ross (2014), these stages help grieving people identify their emotions and unpack their experiences. While they are called stages, they are not intended to be a step-by-step process. It's normal to move through the stages in a different order, to skip a stage and perhaps circle back to it over time, or to repeat the same stage over and over for a while. Think of these five stages as fluid experiences that come and go throughout your life.

Denial

The first stage of grief involves refusing to believe or acknowledge that something painful occurred at all. Clients in this stage are unable to acknowledge that their parents did anything wrong, or even that they made any mistakes. This may be voluntary or involuntary—some clients simply cannot remember much of their childhood (something we refer to as *dissociation*), while others have a lot of practice choosing not to think or talk about it. I've heard parents in this stage describe really awful memories from their childhood, followed by statements like "But it wasn't that bad," "It could have been worse," or "I may not be remembering things correctly."

Anger

Once a person recognizes how painful their childhood (or some aspects of it) was, they may start to experience profound anger toward their parents, other family members, or God for not protecting them. Parents in this stage often tear up in the therapy room when describing how their parents raised them. Outside of therapy, they might show increased frustration or hostility toward others, including in how they parent their child. This stage of grief can feel very uncomfortable, but it is essential in order for healing to occur.

Bargaining

Bargaining looks like an attempt to negotiate the pain away. Parents who have spiritual or religious beliefs often direct the bargaining toward a higher power: *If God would just make this pain go away, then I could parent my child from a better place.* Another way bargaining can manifest is through "what if" ideation of the past and future: *What if I'd been a better kid? What if I actually caused my abuse?* Parents may also engage in bargaining with their child under the belief that if they get parenting "right," the pain of their own childhood won't seem so bad.

Depression

This is the most recognizable stage of grief, characterized by deep sadness and a feeling of emptiness left by the loss or lack of something precious. A parent may go through this stage when they consciously recognize that their childhood cannot be recovered or the pain repaired. It's not uncommon for parents to experience depression while raising their own child because it reminds them of the childhood they missed out on. It can be especially triggering when their child doesn't acknowledge how good they have it or thank their parent for raising them the "correct" way. These parents want their child to enjoy their childhood and never be upset, the way they often were during their own painful childhood. This stage of grief can prompt harmful parenting patterns, such as covering up the depression by neglecting to set boundaries or consequences, or attempting to remake the parent-child relationship into a "friendship" that feeds the parent's need for acceptance and minimizes conflict.

Acceptance

The final stage of grief is the point at which the many intense emotions start to plateau, as parents realize the past cannot be changed. To be clear, acceptance is not saying it's okay that your parents neglected or hurt you; rather, it's recognizing that although you suffered pain, you're going to be okay. During this stage, parents become able to acknowledge past experiences and grieve their losses, allowing them to focus on their child's needs in their parenting decisions. Rather than attempting to be everything or provide everything for their child in the hope of repairing their own pain, these parents learn to be more present and make the most of each day by parenting the child they have, not the child they were.

Children with Disabilities

In 2012, I began specializing in treating families who are raising a child with a disability. A big part of working with these parents is teaching them about grieving the loss of the able-bodied or neurotypical child they thought they would have. Raising a child with a disability can be a lifetime of happiness as well as losses. For example, a parent who rose to the challenge of their child's diagnosis may still find themselves grieving when they are told that their child is not cognitively ready to enter the next grade level and has to repeat the same grade. Even parents who feel content with their family and proud of their child with a disability may grieve when they see other children walking by themselves, graduating from high school, or getting married, as they acknowledge that their child may never experience those same events.

If you're raising a child with a disability, I highly recommend you seek out a therapist to help you navigate the complex emotions you may experience. The five stages of grief are still a good starting point, but learning more about your unique situation can help you reach a deeper level of healing.

Activity 12.2
Processing Grief

This activity will help you explore how the five stages of grief might resonate with your experience of grieving the child or childhood you wish you had. Acknowledging all of your feelings, rather than trying to suppress them, will allow you to move forward through the grief process. Remember, these stages are not a step-by-step guide, but fluid experiences that you may move between in any order, with any number of repetitions, throughout your life.

Denial

Signs of being in the denial stage include not remembering much of your childhood, questioning the accuracy of your memories, believing that your parents are infallible (that they didn't make *any* mistakes or harmful choices), or feeling like you don't have the right to disagree with your parents or to feel hurt by them. Have you experienced any of these signs in the past (or perhaps recently)? Describe your experience.

_____

_____

_____

_____

_____

_____

_____

Anger

Is there anyone you feel deeply or consistently angry with—whether it's your parent, another family member, a higher power, or someone else? What do you do or say when you feel this anger?

_____

_____

_____

_____

_____

_____

_____

_____

If the responses you've described are not helpful to you and others (e.g., yelling at your loved ones or trying to bottle up your anger), read the following list of coping activities and circle a few that you'd like to try:

- Journaling about your feelings

- Deep breathing exercises

- Exercising (walking, yoga, etc.)

- Listening to music

- Housework (cleaning, gardening, etc.)

- Talking with a trusted person

- Playing with your child or pet

- Watching or listening to your favorite comedy show

- Add your own: _____

Bargaining

The bargaining stage often involves "what if" or "if only" thoughts, such as, *What if I'd been able to meet my parents' expectations?* or *If only my child would do what I say, then their life would be perfect.* Do you ever have thoughts like these? Describe them.

_____

_____

_____

_____

_____

_____

_____

What do these thoughts suggest about your unmet needs? About your child's needs?

_____

_____

_____

_____

_____

_____

_____

_____

Depression

This stage is characterized by deep sadness and the feeling of lacking or having lost something precious. Do you ever feel this way? Describe the events or memories that trigger these feelings.

How are these feelings affecting you? How are they influencing the way you parent your child?

Acceptance

Acknowledging your past experiences and grieving your losses will allow you to be more present and to focus on your child's needs in your parenting decisions. Try writing an affirmation that honors your resilience and growth—for example, *I am strong enough to face challenges* or *I am working hard to be the parent my child needs.* Repeat your affirmation several times a day to establish a positive thought pattern. You've got this!

Trust the Process

Grieving can be a complicated process, one that you may be working through all your life. It doesn't make you a bad person if you've wondered what it would have been like to have a different child or childhood. However, trying to answer that question by parenting your child the way you wish you'd been parented will not create a healthy, resilient relationship with your child. Parenting the child you have is only possible once you begin healing from your past traumas and unmet needs. While this process may take months or years of self-reflection, therapy, and practice in meeting your own needs, I have personally witnessed parents just like you experience deeper, more meaningful relationships with their child within weeks of allowing themselves to acknowledge and begin processing their grief.

Chapter 13

—

Embracing the Unique Child You Have

Learning to parent is a lifelong process, and so is healing from your past. Since you may not reach complete healing before your parenting days are over, it's important to identify ways you can bond with your child even as you learn to parent better. Each section in this final chapter offers different ways you can deepen your connection, improve your communication, and think about how you love, laugh with, discipline, and respect the amazing child you have.

Loving Your Child

Remember the five love languages we explored in chapter 5? Those love languages have also been researched for and applied to children. Identifying your child's love language may be the most important aspect of parenting, as it helps you communicate love in the primary way your child understands it.

Although you may think your child knows you love them, they may not always perceive or believe it because of the way you attempt to show it. For example, if your child's main love language is physical touch, but you rarely snuggle, rub their back, or give them kisses goodnight, they'll struggle to believe your love for them. I recommend reading *The Five Love Languages of Children* (Chapman & Campbell, 1997), and taking the associated quiz at https://5lovelanguages.com, to help you identify the primary way your child receives love—physical touch, quality time, gifts, words of affirmation, or acts of service.

While most children between the ages of two and twelve will have two or three love languages, you may be able to identify your child's primary love language by asking them to share memories of times when they felt really loved by you. To simplify it, try asking it like this: "What is one of your favorite memories of us? What were you doing, what was I doing, and what about it made you feel the best?"

If your child struggles to identify past events, you can learn about their love languages by giving them several options for future outings together and making each outing idea correspond to a love language—such as going on an ice cream date (quality time) versus helping them clean their room (acts of service) versus writing them a sweet note (words of affirmation).

Once you've identified your child's primary love language, start spending at least ten minutes a day intentionally communicating to them in that language. Many parents object that they don't have ten minutes a day to bond with their child. Unfortunately, not having the time isn't an option—not if you want a loving relationship with your child. Children who don't feel their parents' love will attempt to engage them in the most undesirable ways, such as lashing out, yelling, and withdrawing—after all, negative attention is still attention. Life is busy and full of responsibilities, but taking additional time to nourish your relationship will actually make it easier for you to manage other responsibilities. Think about it: When you're making dinner and your child starts interrupting in an effort to receive your attention, it takes you longer to finish than if you had previously spent some time attending to your child and could then make dinner uninterrupted.

One final exercise I suggest doing is to have your child draw an outline of a container—like a gas tank, bottle, or bucket—and then ask your child each day to point to a level on the container to show how full their "love tank" is. Follow it up by asking them, "How can we fill it higher?" You'll be surprised how easily your child will communicate with you about what they need if given the opportunity. Along with making it much easier to meet their needs by eliminating the guesswork, it's the simplest and most powerful way to let your child know that you love them, no matter what their love language is.

Connecting With Your Child

Life can go by incredibly fast. One moment you're chasing after your toddler, and the next moment they're a teenager about to leave the nest! If you don't make an effort to connect with your child on a daily basis, the years can slip away. It's important to make the time to connect with your child no matter what's going on or how they're behaving—not only when they're doing well or celebrating an achievement, but also when they're struggling with big emotions or behaviors and need help finding other options, making different decisions, or self-soothing. Connecting with your child should occur on several levels: emotional, psychological, and physical.

Emotional Connection

Emotional connection is the ability to help your child share and process their feelings with you. To enhance the emotional connection you have with your child, start by asking them how they're feeling at various times throughout the week. This helps your child learn to slow down their thought process and identify what they're actually feeling. If your child can only articulate a handful of emotions, use this as an opportunity to teach them about different emotions and explore how they might experience each one. Once your child can identify a variety of emotions, ask them to tell you about times when they felt a specific emotion and why they believe they felt it. Learning to think about the "why" helps them cultivate the instinct to slow down and reflect when their emotions are activated.

In addition, I always recommend letting your child experience any emotion they're having. Telling your child they *shouldn't* feel a certain way can quickly shut down any openness they have with you. By the same token, never laugh at or dismiss feelings you believe are silly or an overreaction. For example, Carmen once brought home a C on a quiz and cried as she showed it to her parents. Her father rolled his eyes and said, "It's only one C. What are you so upset about?" Carmen came into my office ten years later because she was struggling to share her emotions with her significant other, thanks to a lifetime of having her feelings dismissed in moments such as those. Children need to be assured that it's normal and okay to have any emotion, not just the happy or pleasant ones. Sharing, expressing, and talking about emotions will deepen the connection you have with your child.

Psychological Connection

Psychological connection is a powerful bond you can create with your child through moments of mental togetherness, like laughing at a movie, playing on the same team, and doing projects or solving problems together. These experiences make your child feel closer to you and give them an opportunity to share their experiences and thoughts with you. Here are just a few ways to create those moments of mental togetherness:

- **Ask your child to teach you something.** The activity should be chosen by your child, and you have to actively participate. No multitasking, no other children, and no screens are allowed. This is strictly one-on-one time together. You may be surprised by what you can learn from—and about—your child when you ask.

- **Compliment your child on specific things you see them doing.** Commending your child for characteristics is much more powerful and meaningful than complimenting them on the result. If your child scores a goal in their next soccer game, ask them to tell you *how* they scored the goal. Was it through determination? Playing like a team? Commitment to practicing? Rather than focusing on a successful outcome, acknowledge the characteristics and behaviors it took to achieve it.

- **Be present when things are pleasant.** I don't endorse the *I leave my kids alone when they are being good by themselves* philosophy. Instead, I encourage you to join in on your child's good behavior—reward them with your attention for being calm and well behaved. Show them that people enjoy being around them when they're being sweet, kind, and fun. Plus, studies show that when two people laugh, smile, and share positive emotions together, their brain waves synchronize, causing their minds to connect on a physical level (Nummenmaa et al., 2012).

Physical Connection

Finally, physical connection can strengthen the bond you have with your child. Did you know that hugging your child for thirty seconds can reduce their heart rate? Or that staring into your child's eyes for over thirty seconds can increase their feel-good endorphins? Physical connection can encourage psychological connection as well. Along with hugs, kisses, and tickles, there are many physical activities you can enjoy together—such as playing on a swing set, jumping on a trampoline, or playing a board game—that will connect your minds through smiling and laughter.

Laughing with Your Child

Laughing together is such a wonderful way to strengthen your relationship with your child that it merits its own discussion. Laughter is a powerful stress-relieving activity that, when done with another person, enhances your emotional and psychological connection. To be clear, I am *not* endorsing laughing if what your child is doing is not intended to be funny. This can cause severe embarrassment for your child and make them feel judged. Rather, I am encouraging you to laugh together in moments of play and connection.

There are many ways you can create opportunities to laugh with your child. For younger children, use silly voices or make funny faces when reading books together. Ask your child what kind of voice they think a character may have, then ask them to try to speak like that character. Make sound effects and do silly things when you're playing together that not only create laughter but also trigger their imagination.

As your child ages, you'll need to get more creative with how you cultivate laughter with them. While the default for many teens is to find their parents embarrassing, don't let that stop you from finding opportunities to play with them. The parent-tested techniques I've learned about include visiting theme parks, playing arcade games, or watching comedy movies together. Some parents tell me they text memes and jokes back and forth with their teenagers. No matter how it comes about, laughing, smiling, and appreciating fun (and funniness) together will increase everyone's dopamine levels, strengthening your mental connection and emotional bond.

Disciplining Your Child

Our society teaches parents that they should have control over their children and exert power when their child misbehaves. As a result, the word *discipline* has become synonymous with spanking, time-outs, removing screen time, and being grounded—punishments that emphasize the parent's power and control, which misses the point of discipline altogether. Scolding, hurting, or manipulating a child doesn't ultimately correct their behavior; the only long-term result is making the child feel disconnected, humiliated, and shameful.

Spanking in particular has been shown to negatively impact the relationship you have with your child (Thompson Gershoff, 2002). It can also cause aggressive behavior—children who are hit or spanked are more likely to hit others in close relationships when they are older, such as their children or significant others (Turns & Sibley, 2018). The research confirms what should be common sense. When a child is hit by someone who is supposed to love them, why wouldn't they treat others the same? If you hit your child in response to disobedience or disrespect, you're neither showing nor teaching them the behavior you want to see from them.

While I am not recommending that you remove discipline and consequences from your parenting altogether, I encourage you to shift your definition of discipline from *punishing* your child to *teaching* them. I advocate for using "time-ins" to teach children a more appropriate response than the undesirable behavior they are exhibiting. When toddlers are learning how to play and share with others, they typically hit, yell, or push others to get what they want, simply because they aren't yet aware of their other options. Rather than spanking your child, removing them from the situation, or taking their toy away, try sitting with them and reflecting what they're feeling back to them: "I see you're upset and you really want to play with the doll." Next, show them the behavior that is more appropriate: "Let's ask if we can play with it next." Since toddlers struggle with learning things right away, don't be surprised if this needs to be repeated a few times.

I also encourage you to reward your child for the behaviors you would like to see more of. If your child is playing nicely with others, take a moment to celebrate it and compliment them: "Wow! I love how you're sharing and taking turns. That makes for a good friend." This affirmation helps your child learn what gets positive attention from you, which makes them more likely to repeat the behavior in the future.

As children age, many parents begin disciplining by removing desired items (such as phones, tablets, and cars). Although this may be effective in the short term, the primary purpose of discipline is to teach. Removing property teaches your child nothing specific, only that you have power and control over them. You shouldn't take something away without a legitimate explanation as to why you're removing it and the desired behaviors you would like to see before they get it back. For example, a couple recently came to me because their teen daughter had been sending nude photos to her boyfriend. The parents decided to confiscate her phone for three weeks. However, apart from telling her to give up her phone, they hadn't communicated about the situation at all. I recommended they sit down with their daughter and explain why the seriousness of her actions warranted removing the phone, rather than assuming she already understands.

Respecting Your Child

Although so many parents believe that they have a unilateral right to respect from their children, respect isn't a one-way street within parent-child relationships. If you want your child to respect you, you must respect them as well.

In toddlerhood, you can respect your child by asking their permission for physical touch (even hugs and kisses), entering their personal space, or playing with their toys. While toddlers can be irresistibly cute and snuggly, assuming your toddler wants to be close to you is a common mistake. Since children will copy your behavior, showing respect for their wishes and space by asking their permission is teaching them to respect both themselves and others. I also advise that you don't force your child to give anyone a hug or kiss; instead, allow them to decide by asking, "Would you like to give a hug goodbye?" and then respecting their choice.

Respect also comes in the form of being heard and listened to. If you're struggling with your child not listening to you, think about whether you have been listening to them. Have you heard and understood your child's perspective? Have you asked about their specific needs, wants, and wishes? Many adults who struggle with hearing from others with different values and opinions were rarely listened to by their parents. You don't have to agree with what your child is saying, but you should at least hear and acknowledge their opinions. This will encourage your child to not only listen to you, but also listen to others and develop the ability to hear different views and values without leaving their window of tolerance or needing to defend their own views.

How you speak to your child can be a powerful portrayal of respect—or lack thereof. Do you speak to your child with sarcasm or a condescending tone? Are the words you use accusatory or harsh? If so, expect to hear it back from them. Children will model the words as well as the tone, pitch, and volume that are presented to them. I recommend avoiding condescending and accusatory phrases such as "What do you think you're doing?" "What's wrong with you?" "Why do you think that's okay?" "Where do you think you're going?" and "I raised you better than that." None of these phrases convey respect for your child's opinion, behavior, or thought process. Instead, they all communicate something like this: "You are making a terrible choice and I don't care what your reason is; it's the wrong one."

Finally, respect also comes in the form of privacy. Social media, for all its benefits, has undeniably increased respect issues between parents and children. While parents may share photos or stories of their young child with innocent intentions, those children may not appreciate certain images or descriptions (e.g., being naked in the bathtub, wearing embarrassing clothes, throwing a tantrum) being available for everyone (or even just friends and family) to see. Respect your child's privacy by limiting your posts until your child is able to give permission for sharing them, which should be around twelve years of age.

The topic of privacy always brings questions from parents about boundaries regarding their child's phone. Some never review their child's internet searches, messages, or social media content, while others look at their child's phone every night. Each child is going to need a different set of boundaries that lie somewhere between the two extremes. I do recommend that parents discuss social media safety with their children, particularly the importance of never posting or writing a message they wouldn't want to be seen by everyone, including strangers. I also recommend sitting with your child when you review their phone so that you can discuss any potential issues you see and give your child the opportunity to respond. As your child ages, the amount of time you spend reviewing their content should decrease as your trust for them increases.

Activity 13.1
Bonding with Your Child

This activity will help you identify ways you're currently connecting with, disciplining, and respecting your child. Acknowledging these will help you recognize intentional ways you are working toward a stronger relationship with your child. You may also recognize areas that you would like to change in order to better meet your child's needs.

In what ways are you currently connecting with your child?

What are your typical forms of discipline?

How do you show your child respect?

Do you see any overlap between the ways you connect with, discipline, and respect your child and the way you were raised?

_____

_____

_____

_____

What are a few new ways you would like to start bonding with your child?

_____

_____

_____

_____

Are there more useful forms of discipline you would like to try?

_____

_____

_____

_____

How would you like to show your child respect?

_____

_____

_____

_____

Connections Last Forever

When working with parents, I often remind them that the way they connect with, treat, and discipline their child will become a voice in the child's mind. For instance, if you rarely ask about your child's interests or hobbies, they will likely grow up thinking their pastimes and pursuits are not worthy or important. But if you show your child that you want to learn about who they are, that you enjoy spending time with them, and that you respect them, they will believe that they are an important person who is worthy of someone's love and attention. Although it can be challenging to monitor every interaction you have with your child, try to enhance at least one interface and watch how quickly your relationship with them will flourish.

Final Remarks

After over a decade as a family therapist, I'm convinced that parenting is the hardest job in the world. Parenting the child you have, not the child you were, is a new way of thinking about this job, not to mention a complex process. No one expects you to get it right all the time, and you shouldn't expect this from yourself, either.

I'm proud of you for sticking with this journey of exploring and improving your parenting habits. It takes a lot of courage to face your trauma, comfort your inner child, and embrace the challenges you've experienced. Not only are you healing yourself and protecting your child—you're also protecting their potential children by breaking generational patterns.

I've seen time and time again that when parents are willing to invest time and energy into learning how to parent more effectively, the entire family benefits. By actively practicing these skills, you're giving your family a gift of healing that can last for generations.

Appendix

List of Characteristics

Autonomy	Grace	Peace	Self-care
Compassion	Gratitude	Persistence	Self-control
Consistency	Honesty	Playfulness	Support
Contentment	Humility	Predictability	Tolerance
Cooperation	Humor	Presence	Trustworthiness
Creativity	Intelligence	Resilience	Understanding
Curiosity	Intentionality	Respect	Wisdom
Dependability	Kindness	Responsibility	Work ethic
Encouragement	Optimism	Rest	
Flexibility	Patience	Self-awareness	

List of Emotions

Angry	Exhausted	Hesitant	Respectful
Anxious	Fearful	Horrified	Scared
Awestruck	Flustered	Inspired	Sad
Brave	Frustrated	Joyful	Shy
Calm	Fulfilled	Mad	Silly
Curious	Funny	Manipulative	Surprised
Disappointed	Glad	Moody	Thoughtful
Disrespected	Grateful	Motivated	Threatened
Embarrassed	Greedy	Nervous	Timid
Empathetic	Guilty	Overstimulated	Upset
Enraged	Happy	Powerful	
Excited	Heartbroken	Proud	

List of Behaviors

Apologizing	Kissing	Setting limits
Asking	Laughing	Sharing
Confirming	Listening	Showing respect
Deep breathing	Nodding	Sitting quietly
Doing work	Playing	Smiling
Eating healthy	Praising	Snuggling
Following directions	Providing boundaries	Talking
Giving choices	Replying	Telling
Helping	Resting	Writing
Holding	Rocking	
Hugging	Scheduling time	

References

Bowen, H. J., Kark, S. M., & Kensinger, E. A. (2017). NEVER forget: Negative emotional valence enhances recapitulation. *Psychonomic Bulletin & Review, 25*(3), 870–981. https://doi .org/10.3758%2Fs13423-017-1313-9

Burns, A., Homel, R., & Goodnow, J. J. (1984). Conditions of life and parental values. *Australian Journal of Psychology, 36*(2), 219–237. https://doi.org/10.1080/00049538408255093

Canli, T., Zhao, Z., Brewer, J., Gabrieli, J. D., & Cahill, L. (2000). Event-related activation in the human amygdala associates with later memory for individual emotional experience. *Journal of Neuroscience, 20*(19), 1–5. https://doi.org/10.1523/jneurosci.20 -19-j0004.2000

Chapman, G. (2014). *The 5 love languages singles edition.* Northfield Publishing.

Chapman, G. (2015). *The 5 love languages: The secret to love that lasts.* Northfield Publishing.

Chapman, G., & Campbell, R. (1997). *The five love languages of children.* Moody Press.

Dix, T. (1992). Parenting on behalf of the child: Empathic goals in the regulation of responsive parenting. In I. E. Sigel, A. V. McGillicuddy-DeLisi, & J. J. Goodnow (Eds.), *Parental belief systems: The psychological consequences for children* (pp. 319–346). Lawrence Erlbaum Associates, Inc.

Dweck, C. S. (2016). *Mindset: The new psychology of success* (Updated ed.). Ballantine Books.

Gondoli, D. M., & Silverberg, S. B. (1997). Maternal emotional distress and diminished responsiveness: The mediating role of parenting efficacy and parental perspective taking. *Developmental Psychology, 33*(5), 861–868. https://doi.org/10.1037//0012-1649 .33.5.861

Hastings, P. D., & Grusec, J. E. (1998). Parenting goals as organizers of responses to parent–child disagreement. *Developmental Psychology, 34*(3), 465–479. https://doi.org/10.1037/0012-1649.34.3.465

Krauss, S., Orth, U., & Robins, R. W. (2020). Family environment and self-esteem development: A longitudinal study from age 10 to 16. *Journal of Personality and Social Psychology, 119*(2), 457–478. https://doi.org/10.1037%2Fspp0000263

Kübler-Ross, E. (2014). *On death and dying: What the dying have to teach doctors, nurses, clergy & their own families* (50th anniversary ed.). Scribner Publishing.

Nummenmaa, L., Glerean, E., Viinikainen, M., Jääskeläinen, I. P., Hari, R., & Sams, M. (2012). Emotions promote social interaction by synchronizing brain activity across individuals. *Proceedings of the National Academy of Sciences, 109*(24), 9599 –9604. https://doi.org/10.1073/pnas.1206095109

Orth, U. (2018). The family environment in early childhood has a long-term effect on self-esteem: A longitudinal study from birth to age 27 years. *Journal of Personality and Social Psychology, 114*(4), 637–655. https://doi.org/10.1037/pspp0000143

Shapiro, F. (2018). *Eye movement desensitization and reprocessing (EMDR) therapy: Basic principles, protocols, and procedures* (3rd ed.). Guilford Press.

Siegel, D. J. (1999). *The developing mind: How relationships and the brain interact to shape who we are.* Guilford Press.

Siegel, D. J., & Hartzell, M. (2003). *Parenting from the inside out: How a deeper self-understanding can help you raise children who thrive.* Penguin.

Thompson Gershoff, E. (2002). Corporal punishment by parents and associated child behaviors and experiences: A meta-analytic and theoretical review. *Psychological Bulletin, 128*(4), 539–579. https://doi.org/10.1037/0033-2909.128.4.539

Tseng, J., & Poppenk, J. (2020). Brain meta-state transitions demarcate thoughts across task contexts exposing the mental noise of trait neuroticism. *Nature Communications, 11,* Article 3480, 1–12. https://doi.org/10.1038/s41467-020-17255-9

Turns, B. A., & Sibley, D. S. (2018). Does maternal spanking lead to bullying behaviors at school? A longitudinal study. *Journal of Child and Family Studies, 27*(9), 2824–2832. https://doi.org/10.1007/s10826-018-1129-x

Umaña-Taylor, A. J., Guimond, A. B., Updegraff, K. A., & Jahromi, L. B. (2013). A longitudinal examination of support, self-esteem, and Mexican-origin adolescent mothers' parenting efficacy. *Journal of Marriage and Family, 75*(3), 746–759. https://psycnet.apa.org/doi/10.1111/jomf.12019

Wuyts, D., Vansteenkiste, M., Soenens, B., & Assor, A. (2015). An examination of the dynamics involved in parental child-invested contingent self-esteem. *Parenting: Science and Practice, 15*(2), 55–74. https://doi.org/10.1080/15295192.2015.1020135